YOUR CATHOLIC FAITH

D1013706

Your Catholic Faith
A Question-and-Answer Catechism

Alan Schreck
with Wendy Leifeld

Servant Publications
Ann Arbor, Michigan

The Scripture quotations contained herein are from the
Revised Standard Version of the Bible, Catholic edition,
copyright 1965 and 1966 by the Division of Christian
Education of the National Council of the Churches of
Christ in the U.S.A., and are used by permission.

Redeemer Books is an imprint of Servant Publications
especially designed to serve Catholics.

Published by Servant Publications
P.O. Box 8617
Ann Arbor, Michigan 48107

Cover design by Michael Andaloro
Cover photograph of silhouetted church by Albert
Normandin/The Image Bank

Printed in the United States of America
ISBN 0-89283-627-X

    90 91 92 93 94 10 9 8 7 6 5 4 3 2

Nihil Obstat: Monsignor Joseph P. Malara
                Censor Librorum
Imprimatur: † Most Reverend Albert H. Ottenweller
                Bishop of Steubenville
March 17, 1989

The *nihil obstat* and *imprimatur* are official declarations that a
book or pamphlet is free from doctrinal or moral error. No
implication is contained therein that *those who grant the nihil
obstat* or *imprimatur* agree with the contents, opinions, or
statements expressed.

Library of Congress Cataloging-in-Publication Data

Schreck, Alan
    Your Catholic Faith : a question-and-answer catechism /
by Alan Schreck with Wendy Leifeld.
        p. cm.
    Includes index.
    ISBN 0-89283-627-X
    1. Catholic Church—Catechism—English. I. Leifeld,
Wendy. II. Title.
BX1961.S37   1989
238'.2—dc20
                                        89-10147
                                          CIP

TABLE OF CONTENTS

Introduction / 7

1. God, Creation, and the Fall / 11
2. God's Plan of Salvation / 21
3. The Church / 39
4. How God Reveals Himself / 57
5. The Sacraments / 69
6. Prayer, Devotions, and the Holy Spirit / 91
7. Living as a Catholic Christian / 105
8. Catholics in the World / 121
9. Mary / 131
10. The Life of the Age to Come / 139

Appendices
   Appendix One: Glossary of Terms Italicized in
      Text / 149
   Appendix Two: Some Commonly Recited Catholic
      Prayers / 153
Index / 159

How to Use This Catechism

Pope John Paul II wrote in *Familiaris Consortio* (*The Role of the Christian Family in the Modern World*), "In order that Christian parents may worthily carry out their ministry of educating, the Synod Fathers expressed the hope that a suitable *Catechism for Families* would be prepared, one that would be clear, brief, and easily assimilated by all" (No. 39). Guided by this exhortation, we have set to work on this catechism for families, catechists, and others. Indeed, the Holy Father has encouraged the laity to take up this task. In *Christi Fideles Laici* (*The Lay Members of Christ's Faithful People*), Pope John Paul writes:

> In the case of coming generations, the lay faithful must offer the very valuable contribution, more necessary than ever, of a *systematic work in catechesis*. The Synod Fathers have gratefully taken note of the work of catechists, acknowledging that they "have a task that is of great importance in animating ecclesial communities." . . . we all ought to be aware of the "rights" that each baptized person has to be instructed, educated, and supported in the faith and the Christian life. (No. 34)

Inspired and informed by the Holy Father's vision, this book is a question-and-answer catechism that draws upon *Basics of the Faith*, a longer catechism by Alan Schreck (Servant Publications, 1987). The question-and-answer format allows individuals and families to locate quickly and answer the kinds of questions Catholics frequently ask about their faith.

This catechism has been specifically designed to be used by parents, catechists, and others to increase their own understanding and provide simple explanations about the faith for children, teenagers, and adults. It will prove especially helpful to parents on occasions when children and teenagers begin to ask questions about their faith.

The material is largely adapted from *Basics of the Faith*. However, this catechism is not a study guide or companion volume. It can be used profitably by itself. The answers were not developed in order to be memorized but to give enough information so that the reader or presenter understands the concept adequately.

The numbers in italic typeface at the end of most of the answers refer to page numbers in *Basics of the Faith* where a fuller treatment of the subject is given. Wherever pertinent, scriptural references are also given for further study. Some terms are italicized when they first appear in the text. These terms are defined in the short glossary at the end of the book, unless they are fully defined in the text.

In addition, a collection of some commonly recited Catholic prayers ends the book. These prayers touch upon many aspects mentioned in the catechism—the Trinity, the communion of saints, the family, thanksgiving, the angels, and the Mother of God. They are ideal for beginning and ending a catechetical session or a family discussion with prayer. These prayers can also be used for recitation and memorization in other settings, such as morning and evening prayer.

Every Catholic family, parochial school library, and parish library will find this basic primer of the faith a valuable resource. Its simple format makes it practical for both quick and more in-depth reference, especially in day-to-day instruction of children and teenagers. All the essentials of the faith—as well as commonly asked questions concerning Catholic doctrines—are provided, making it appropriate for use by all who are interested in a basic understanding of Catholicism.

ONE

God, His Creation, and the Fall

God

1. How do we know there is a God?
There are two ways that we can come to know that God exists, and what he is like: through natural revelation and through divine revelation. *3*

2. What is "natural revelation"?
Through observing and thinking about the universe we can come to know certain things about God (Ps 19:1; Rom 1:20). This is called natural revelation. When we look at the stars, the immensity of the ocean, or one solitary snow-flake, we know something greater than these must have made them. *3*

3. What is "divine revelation"?
The second and more complete way of coming to know God is by divine revelation. Human beings could never come to know the full truth about God through nature. In order that we might know him clearly, God has revealed himself and his mind to us through the Scriptures and through the teaching of the apostles and of the church, inspired by the Holy Spirit. The fullness of divine revela-

tion is the coming of God himself among us as a man, Jesus Christ (Heb 1:1–2). 4–5

4. How do we know that this knowledge is true?
This kind of knowledge cannot be proven by reason or scientific investigation. Ultimately, we only know with assurance that God has spoken and revealed himself to us through faith. We believe the writings and witnesses who testify that God has spoken and made himself known. 5

We also recognize it is true because it corresponds to our own experience in life. For example, our personal struggles with sin can make it painfully clear that we need a Savior, someone to reconcile us with ourselves, to one another, and with God. 5–6

5. What does it mean to have faith in God's revelation?
Faith is a divine gift that illumines God and his presence among us. Scientists use ultraviolet rays to detect things that cannot be seen by the naked eye. Faith is a light that enables us to see and know God and spiritual reality that we cannot perceive by our own unaided reason or senses.

6. What is God like?
The foundational truth about God is that there is one, and only one, God (Dt 6:4). 6

7. Is there any other being equal to God?
No. The teaching of Jesus in the Gospels reaffirm that there is only one God (Mk 12:29), who alone is all-powerful, all-knowing, and perfect in goodness and in love. We can let other things or ideas have dominion over us, but that does not make them equal in power or authority to the one true God (Is 45:22–24). 6–7

8. What is God?
"God is spirit" (Jn 4:24). God does not have a brain nor any

other material part, yet he possesses intellect and free will, the ability to think and reason, to choose and decide. He is pure, unbounded spirit. However, this doesn't make him an impersonal cosmic force or set of ideals. Though God is spirit, he is a person. Christians believe that God is a person *like us* in many ways, because we are made in God's image and likeness. However, God is also *unlike* us in his purely spiritual nature and in the perfection of his power, goodness, beauty, and all desirable attributes. To paraphrase St. Anselm, God is that which is better and greater than anything we can think of or imagine. *9–10*

9. What does it mean that God is a person if he is not a human being?
God is the ultimate source and model of what a person is. We are persons because we are made in the image and likeness of God. We have some idea of what it means to be a person (Gn 1:26) because we know ourselves. *10–11*

10. Is God one, or is he three?
God is one because he possesses a single divine nature, the nature of God. Through divine revelation we know that the one God exists as three persons who are distinct but undivided, since each person fully possesses the same divine nature, the nature of God. God as three yet one is called the blessed Trinity. St. Patrick is said to have taught about the blessed Trinity by pointing to a single shamrock (representing the one God) possessing three equal leaves (the three persons). *11–13*

11. If they all have the same nature, are the three persons of God identical, like "clones" of the same person?
No, they are not identical. Each person of the Trinity is a person in a particular and unique way. The Father is the ultimate origin or source of the other persons of the Trinity, and only he sent the Son into the world. Only God the

Son became man in order to save us from sin and reveal his Father in heaven. Only the Spirit is sent into our hearts by the Father and the Son as God's gift of love and power dwelling within us.

Though they are not identical, the persons of God are united so deeply that Jesus could say to Philip, "He who has seen me has seen the Father" (Jn 14:9). Elsewhere Jesus teaches that the Holy Spirit only will reveal what belongs to the Father and the Son (Jn 16:14, 15). *12*

12. How do we know there is a Trinity at all?
God chose to reveal the secrets of his inner life through Jesus Christ, especially through the great passages on the Trinity in the Gospel of John (Jn 10:30; 14:11; 15:26). Through faith in this revelation, we have a deeper grasp of this truth about God. Studying Scripture and the writings of the church fathers can lead us to a fuller appreciation and understanding of this mystery. *12–13*

13. What is the greatest attribute of God?
The greatest attribute of God is love. The Bible repeatedly testifies that the inner life of God—the Father, the Son, and the Holy Spirit—is especially characterized by mutual love (Jn 12:27, 28, 49, 50; Mt 3:17; 1 Cor 12:3). The first Letter of John even states that "God is love." God's love is not a passing emotion or feeling, nor is it a love that allows unrepented injustice, sin, or rebellion to go unpunished. God's merciful love does not contradict his justice. Jesus's life and example shows that love involves obedience (Jn 14:21). *13–14*

Creation

14. Why did God create the universe?
Because God is love. It is the nature of love to express itself, to give of itself. Out of God's desire to express him-

self and to give of himself out of sheer love, the universe came into existence. Just as the love of a married couple is made visible through the new life of a child, so the overflowing love of God is manifested in his creation. *14–16*

15. What do we mean by "creation," or the "created universe"?
To create means to produce something out of nothing, whether it is material or spiritual. Only God can create— he is *the* creator. God created all things: matter, energy, and even time. *16*

16. How did creation begin?
The Catholic church does not teach one view of precisely how and when God created the universe, but insists that God is the author of creation. Catholics may accept any scientific theory of the origin of the cosmos as long as it does not deny that God is finally, and ultimately, the source and creator of all that exists. *25*

17. What are angels? Are they part of creation?
The Greek word *angelos* means "messenger." They are pure spirits, like God himself, possessing understanding and free will. At their creation, all the angels were perfectly good and loving. They were created before the universe to give glory to God and to serve God's will and purposes (Heb 1:6, 14). In the Bible, God often sent angels as messengers to humanity, to bear important truths or commands. *16*

18. Was Satan created by God?
God created Satan as an angel who was totally good and one of God's most magnificent creatures. However, in his pride, Satan desired to be equal to God, his creator. This sin of pride drove him to rebellion against God. He has been called by various names in the Bible and Christian

tradition: Lucifer, Satan, the devil. Other angels followed
Satan in his rebellion. By their action they have been de-
prived of heaven; that is why we call them "fallen angels"
(Is 14:12–15; Jude 6; Rv 12:7–9). *17–18*

19. Was evil created by God?
No. Evil actually has no existence of its own; it is a distortion, corruption, or absence of the good that comes from
God. God is totally good, and everything he created is
good (Gn 1:31).

Where did evil come from? God created men and angels
with wills that are free to accept or to reject the good
things and plan of God. The origin of evil was the freely
chosen rebellion of Satan and other angels against God
and his plan. Hence, evil also may be defined as any rebellion against God and his will, and any consequences of
that rebellion.

20. Are good and evil equally powerful?
No. Christianity teaches that good is stronger than evil
and will ultimately triumph over it. God, who is perfect
goodness, has triumphed over the chief power of evil,
Satan, and has condemned him and all who follow him to
an eternity of torment in hell, forever separated from
God's presence (Jude 9; Rv 12:7–9). Satan is not God's
equal. He is the archangel Michael's equal and combatant.
19

21. Why did God make man and woman?
We have been created to find our fulfillment and peace
only in knowing, loving, and serving God. The experience
of all history shows that human beings will be restless and
searching until they have surrendered their lives totally to
God. St. Augustine of Hippo wrote, "You have made us
for Yourself, and our hearts are restless until they rest in
You." The outcome of knowing, loving, and serving God

in our life on earth is that we come to will/know and love God fully for eternity in heaven. This is the destiny that God desires for each person. *8–9*

22. Does the Catholic church believe in evolution?
The Catholic church does not officially teach either the hypothesis that the human race evolved from lower species (evolution) or that mankind was created directly by God (creationism). This is a matter of scientific investigation rather than a matter of faith necessary for salvation. The Catholic church does insist, however, that the human soul or spiritual nature is directly infused by God into each man and woman, beginning with Adam and Eve. There can be no evolution of the soul of any person. *25–26*

23. How do we find our fulfillment and peace in God?
Because we are made in the image and likeness of God, we are called into a relationship with him. We have the capacity to say "yes" or "no" to God because of the capacity for intellectual knowledge and freedom of choice and action. Our peace and fulfillment only come in accepting him and his will for our lives. This is the perfection of man found in the Garden of Eden before the fall. *20*

Sin

24. How did man and woman lose this intimate relationship with God?
Satan tempted the first woman, Eve, to disobey God's command not to eat of the fruit of one particular tree. Adam, in turn, ate of the fruit as well (Gn 3:6). Their pride led Adam and Eve to disobey God. Thus, Satan lured the human race into his own sin of pride. He deceived them into wanting to be like God, on their own terms. They acquired knowledge of good and evil because, for the first

time, they had done evil. This was the first sin of the
human race, the "original sin." 20–21

25. Then what does it mean that we are all born with original sin?

The sin of our first parents had more than personal consequences. It affected the whole human race that would
spring from them. Through original sin evil (rebellion
against God and its effects) was introduced into the history
of our race. Original sin not only refers to the first human
sin but to the condition of separation from God into which
every human person is born. 21

26. How does original sin affect us?

By our own experience we are aware of original sin and its
evil effects. The primary effect of original sin is that we
suffer and die (Rom 5:12; 8:2; Jas 4:1–4). We don't naturally
know God and build a real relationship with him. We see
that children are often selfish and greedy instead of innocent and pure. We have lost other natural gifts that Adam
and Eve enjoyed before their rebellion. We are confronted
daily by the wretchedness of the human condition: vio-
lence, poverty, and extortion, to name but a few. In sum,
the good that God originally intended for humanity has
been lost or corrupted through the evil of original sin. 22

27. How do we "catch" original sin? Is it in our genes?

The Catholic church teaches that original sin is not trans-
mitted merely by example but through an actual corruption or distortion of our common human nature. However,
human nature is essentially good and god-like (Gn 1:27,
31), so it is incorrect to speak of "the total depravity of
man," as do some Christian churches. The goodness in
man is "bent" but not "broken." Original sin is not passed
on as a biological characteristic; but as a corruption or distortion of the inherent goodness of our humanity as it was

created by God. It is an inclination and a drive toward evil, rather than toward the all-good God. Because of original sin we find it easier to choose evil than to choose the good, apart from the grace of God through Jesus Christ. 22

28. What is the root effect of original sin?

An inherited rebelliousness against God and his ways, which the apostle Paul calls "the flesh" (Gal 5:19–21), is the result of original sin. The flesh is the intrinsic drive we all have to fulfill our desires and passions without regard for God or others (Jas 1:13–15). 22–23

29. What were the consequences of the fall?

Genesis 3:12–19 tells us that the main consequence of man's fall is alienation from God—signified by Adam and Eve being cast out of the garden of Eden with an angel barring their return. Humanity, therefore, became subject to sin and death. Other results of the fall are also found in these verses: alienation from one another (vss. 12, 16); our work and bearing children became, instead of easy and painless, sources of struggle and strife (v. 16, 17–19); even nature became "subjected to futility" and in "bondage to decay" (Rom 8:19–22). These scriptural examples still resonate with our experience of life. 23

30. How can a loving God permit this?

In his love, God gave angels and humanity the great gift of free will. In his justice, God has allowed angels, and men and women to experience the consequences of their free choice. For Satan, this meant eternal separation from God—hell. For Adam and Eve, and the whole human race, this means suffering the effects of original sin and ultimately, eternal separation from God (hell), unless this sin is removed. 23

31. But doesn't mercy triumph over justice?

Yes. God's justice is not the last word. Realizing our weakness and limited understanding and because of his great love for us, God showed mercy and promised from the beginning that humanity would have a second chance (Gn 3:15). Through this second chance the sin of Adam and Eve could be removed, healed, and forgiven. The evil effects of their sin could begin to be reversed.

TWO

God's Plan of Salvation

1. Why couldn't God just have forgiven our sin and reconciled humanity to himself simply by saying, "I forgive?"
In his consummate wisdom, God has a perfect plan for drawing the human race back into right relationship with himself. It depends both on God's merciful offer of forgiveness, and on each person's free response to this offer based on faith and trust in God. He desires mankind to freely accept his offer of forgiveness and life. *29–30*

2. How did God go about drawing us back to himself?
The initial stage of God's plan was to form a specific people who would learn to know God and to live according to his will. Through this people, other peoples and eventually the whole human race would come to know who God is, and would learn to love and obey him. A Savior for the whole world would emerge from God's chosen people. *30–31*

3. What does it mean that God formed a specific people?
The Book of Genesis tells the story of how God spoke to our race, beginning with Noah, in order to draw them to himself. He initiated a series of covenants with humanity which became the basis of the relationship between God

and his special people. Through God's action and revelation among these people they came to know him and his ways. *31*

4. What is a covenant?

The word *covenant* was used in the ancient Near East to describe any solemn agreement between two or more parties. The Judaeo-Christian tradition teaches that God made certain covenants with mankind in order to train his chosen people to follow his ways. *31*

5. What were two of these covenants?

The story of Noah (Gn 9) ends with God's solemn agreement never again to attempt to destroy the earth by a flood. The sign of this covenant is the rainbow. *31–32*

God revealed himself to a man named Abraham and made a great covenant with him that set apart all of Abraham's offspring to be a people holy to the Lord. This set in motion God's plan of salvation. The sign of this covenant was that "every male among you shall be circumcised" (Gn 17:10). *32–33*

These two examples teach us three things. First, God alone initiates the covenant, but those he chooses must accept the covenant and cooperate with it. Second, God's covenants with individuals and the whole people of God have a saving purpose. Third, there is often an outward sign (or signs) of the covenant which symbolizes and calls into mind the covenant between God and his people. *32*

6. Did God make a covenant with Moses at Mount Sinai?

Yes. Before Moses, God's covenant with the Hebrew people required their faith in God and obedience to him, but there was no explicitly defined law that governed the life of this people. At Mount Sinai, God instructed the Israelites through Moses:

". . . if you will obey my voice and keep my covenant, you shall be my own possession among all peoples . . . you shall be a kingdom of priests and a holy nation." (Ex 19:5, 6) *36*

Later, the Lord gave Moses the Ten Commandments which were to be the norm of their conduct.

7. What are the Ten Commandments?

1. "I am the LORD, your God . . . you shall have no other gods before me" (Dt 5:6, 7).
2. "You shall not take the name of the LORD your God in vain" (Dt 5:11).
3. "Observe the sabbath day, to keep it holy, as the LORD, your God commanded you; Six days you shall labor, and do all your work; but the seventh day is a sabbath to the LORD your God . . ." (Dt 5:12–14).
4. "Honor your father and your mother, as the LORD your God commanded you, that your days may be prolonged . . ." (Dt 5:16).
5. "You shall not kill" (Dt 5:17).
6. "Neither shall you commit adultery" (Dt 5:18).
7. "Neither shall you steal" (Dt 5:19).
8. "Neither shall you bear false witness against your neighbor" (Dt 5:20).
9. "Neither shall you covet your neighbor's wife" (Dt 5:21).
10. "You shall not desire your neighbor's house, his field, . . . or anything else that is your neighbor's" (Dt 5:21). *37*

8. Are the Ten Commandments arbitrary, externally imposed laws?

No. They set down some of the ways that God had originally created human beings to relate to him and to each other.

9. Did Jesus do away with the Ten Commandments?
No. Jesus insisted that they be obeyed and taught the Jewish people how to interpret them correctly and live them more radically, reaching to the heart of God's commandments: total love of God and love of neighbor (Mt 5:18–19; 19:17–19; 1 Jn 2:3–5; 5:3).

For example Jesus said, "You have heard . . . 'You shall not kill; and whoever kills shall be liable to judgment.' But I say to you that everyone who is angry with his brother shall be liable to judgment . . . whoever says 'You fool!' shall be liable to the hell of fire" (Mt 5:21–22). It is not enough for the disciples of Jesus to avoid doing evil. He taught his followers, for example, that those who were merciful and made peace with one another were blessed (Mt 5:7, 9). *37–38*

10. Did the Israelites faithfully follow this Law?
No. No sooner had Moses delivered the Law than the Hebrews violated the first commandment by making and worshiping a golden calf. In fact, the subsequent history of Israel follows a basic pattern of events that demonstrates the people's need for periodic renewal and conversion:
1. The people sin, violating God's commandments;
2. God allows them to suffer the just punishment of their rebellion;
3. The people cry out to God for mercy and forgiveness;
4. The Lord has compassion, removing the punishment and offering forgiveness;
5. The people repent, turning away from their wrongdoing and returning to obedience to God.

A good example of this cycle is presented by the Book of Judges 2:6–23. *39*

11. How did God call the Israelites back to him?
God raised up the prophets whose mission was to call the

people to repent, to change their evil ways, and turn back to faithfulness to the covenant. 40

12. Don't prophets foretell the future?

They may do this through God's inspiration but the main task of a prophet is to speak God's word for a specific circumstance. Sometimes this word is to give a harsh message of conviction for sin (for violation of the covenant). At other times it is a message of hope and consolation in times of hardship or affliction resulting from the people's sin and lack of faithfulness. The true prophet speaks not his own word but God's word, through the inspiration of the Holy Spirit.

Hosea, a prophet who lived in the northern kingdom of Israel during the seventh century B.C., strongly condemned the people's unfaithfulness to the covenant but also spoke of God's unfailing love and promise of restoration: "Return, O Israel, to the Lord your God, for you have stumbled because of your iniquity . . . I will heal their faithlessness; I will love them freely, for my anger has turned from them" (Hos 14:1, 4). 40

13. What are the messianic prophecies?

These are another step in the unfolding of God's plan of salvation. The prophets helped prepare the people for one who would deliver God's people from bondage. These prophecies, contained in the writings of the Old Testament prophets, foretell the coming of the Messiah, or anointed one, who would deliver Israel from captivity. One of the main prophecies about the Messiah was delivered by the prophet Nathan to King David:

Moreover the LORD declares to you that the LORD will make you a house. When your days are fulfilled and you lie down with your fathers, I will raise up your offspring after you, who shall come forth from your body, and I will establish his kingdom. He shall build a house for my name, and I will establish the throne of his kingdom forever. I will be his father, and he shall be my son. (2 Sm 7:11–14) *40–41*

14. Didn't this refer to his son Solomon?
Yes. Many prophecies have a dual fulfillment. The immediate fulfillment was Solomon who built a house for the Lord, the first great temple in Jerusalem. The deeper fulfillment of the prophecy was the coming of the Messiah, whose rule would last forever, and who is Son of the Father (God) in the fullest sense. *41*

15. How should Christians regard these prophecies?
We believe that God spoke through many of the prophets of the Old Testament to point to and prepare the way for the coming of the true Messiah, Jesus Christ. Jesus is the only one who ultimately fulfills all of the prophecies of the Messiah in the Hebrew Scriptures. *41*

16. What other prophecies in the Old Testament have special meaning for us as Christians?
Some prophecies foretell a new covenant initiated by God that would fulfill and even exceed the promises of God in the former covenant. One of the signs promised by God is the sending of God's Spirit in a new and more powerful way upon the people (Jer 31:31–34; Ez 37:10; Ps 104:29, 30; Jl 3:1–2). Some Old Testament prophecies, such as Daniel 7:13–14, are apocalyptic prophecies that foretell Jesus' second coming and the last judgment of mankind. *42–43*

17. Why don't the Jewish people believe that Jesus is the fulfillment of these prophecies?
God does not impose his designs on anyone; even his chosen people were free to reject the New Covenant. Only a portion, or a remnant, of the Jewish people accepted

Jesus as the Messiah and entered into the New Covenant. The apostle Paul reflects on the meaning of this in Romans 9–11. *43–44*

18. After all this preparation, how did God fulfill his plan of salvation?

God sent his own Son into the world so that all who believed in him would not perish but have eternal life (Jn 3:16). He personally entered into human history to save us from our sin and rebellion and to show us—to demonstrate—his consuming love for us. This is the heart of the good news and the fulfillment of God's plan of salvation. *53*

19. Who is God's Son?

Jesus Christ is the Son of God, possessing fully the nature of God as well as our human nature. The Son or Word of God has always existed with the Father and the Holy Spirit as the Second Person of the Blessed Trinity, but for our salvation he took on human nature and lived among us as a man (Jn 1:1–4; Jn 8:58; Heb 1:1–3). This belief that the Son or Word of God became man is called the incarnation. *51–52*

20. If he is God's Son when was he born?

Many people have asked this same question in the church's history. The Nicene Creed was written to clarify what Christians believe about Christ. Arius, a fourth century theologian, wrongly maintained that since the Son was born of God, there must have been a time when the Son was not—a time before the Son of God existed. The Nicene Creed refuted this heresy. It says that the Son is "eternally begotten" of the Father, which means that there was never a time when the Son or Word of God did not exist. *52*

21. What does it mean that the Son is "God from God, Light from Light, true God from true God, begotten, not made, one in being with the Father. . . ."?

This part of the Nicene Creed was written to further clarify the church's teaching, rejecting Arius' claim that the Son was not God but only the highest creature of God. The creed asserts that the Son of God was begotten or born of God, not "made" or created. The Son is fully God, "one in being" (Greek: *homoousios*) with the Father. Since the Father is God, so is the Son. 52

22. Who created everything that exists, the Father or the Son?

Both the Bible and the creed state that with the Father, the Son of God created all that has been made (Jn 1:3; Heb 1:2). 53

23. How did the incarnation occur? How did God become man?

The Son of God came among us in the flesh by being born of a young Jewish woman of Nazareth named Mary. Thus, he took on the limitations and pains of our human condition (Jn 1:14; Gal 4:4). This is the key to God's plan to redeem the human race from sin and rebellion and to restore us to his friendship. 53–54

24. What does the virgin birth mean?

It means that the Son of God was conceived in the womb of the Virgin Mary solely by the power of the Holy Spirit (Lk 1:27, 31, 35). This fulfills the prophecy in Isaiah 7:14. Jesus had no human father. Joseph is honored by Christians as the guardian, protector, and foster father of Jesus, and head of the Holy Family. Mary is the true, natural mother of Jesus Christ, that is why we call her "Mother of God." 54

25. Was Jesus always the Son of God or did God adopt him?
Jesus was always the Son of God. He was not adopted by God at any point. *56*

26. Is Jesus God or is he man?
The Catholic church has always vigorously affirmed the truth of both Jesus' full divinity and full humanity. Jesus is truly God and truly man. Jesus possesses two distinct but inseparable natures, the divine and the human, united in one person. *54–55*

27. How are these two natures perfectly joined in one person?
Catholic tradition speaks of the "hypostatic union" of the divine and human natures of Jesus, expressing the closest possible union without change or confusion of the natures. How this occurs remains a mystery; all we can say is that they are inseparably joined in the person of Jesus. Creeds and theological definitions can distinguish what is true and what is false, but they can never exhaust the mystery of the reality of God and his plan. *55*

28. Then does Jesus have a "split-personality"—at one moment doing something human, the next moment doing something that only God could do?
No. Those who followed Jesus did not perceive him in this way because these two natures in Jesus worked together in perfect harmony. The Protestant reformer John Calvin proposed that Jesus' two natures functioned together like our two eyes: each eye is distinct, yet they work together in such perfect unison that our vision is one.

29. What did Jesus do?
For the first thirty years he lived the ordinary life of a carpenter's son in the small town of Nazareth in Galilee.

When Jesus was near thirty he went to receive John's baptism (Mt 3:13). John recognized Jesus as the long-awaited Messiah (Jn 1:29). Jesus went into the desert to pray and fast, and he was tempted by Satan. Defeating Satan, he went to Galilee and began to preach the good news of the kingdom of God (Mk 1:14–15). Jesus taught, healed, worked miracles, and cast out demons. Although many became his followers, he was rejected by the leaders of the Jews and condemned to death on a cross. Jesus accepted this death for our salvation. He was crucified and died; on the third day he rose again from the dead. He ascended into heaven and now reigns in glory with God the Father and the Holy Spirit.

30. What is the "good news"?
The good news is that Jesus had come to establish God's reign or rule over people's hearts and lives (Mk 1:14). The kingdom of God isn't a political entity but freedom, through Christ, from everything that prevents God from ruling over our lives. Through the power of Jesus Christ and the Holy Spirit, we are able to love and serve God freely as his sons and daughters and not as slaves. 57

31. When Jesus said that the reign of God was "at hand" (Mk 1:15), did he mean that it was beginning now, or was it to come in the future?
The New Testament indicates that the reign or kingdom of God began with Jesus' own teaching and ministry. Jesus showed the power of God's reign in a number of ways. First, Jesus taught with authority; that is, there was spiritual power in his very words (Mt 7:29). He claimed authority to interpret rightly the whole Jewish law and tradition. Second, he demonstrated his power over Satan and evil spirits (Lk 11:20). Finally, Jesus' mighty works of healing, raising the dead, stilling storms, multiplying food, and

other works were signs that God's kingdom had begun (Mt 11:3–5; Jn 10:24–25, 37–38; Acts 2:22).

However, though the reign of God broke into history with Jesus' public ministry, its completion or fulfillment, when his reign will be evident to all, will not occur until Jesus returns to earth in glory at the end of time. 58–59

32. What did Jesus teach, and how did he teach?
He taught both directly and by parables. The parables are original analogies and stories that teach us about God and his kingdom. Sometimes Jesus described God and his work directly, or described the kind of conduct required of those under God's rule (Mt 13:31; Lk 10:25–37). The beatitudes (Mt 5:1–12; Lk 6:20–26) are an example of how Jesus taught directly about living with and for God. 59–60

33. What did Jesus teach about God, his Father?
First, he taught his followers about God's tremendous love, care, and provision for them in all circumstances (Mt 6:25–34). He taught us to call God our Father, and that we are sons and daughters of God and heirs of the kingdom—if we choose to allow God to rule over our lives. He also taught that God permits us to make our choices freely—even if that means rejecting him. Sometimes it means that we must suffer the consequences of rebellion against him. Jesus perfectly reflected his Father's joy (Lk 15:3–7), sorrow (Lk 19:41–44), and righteous anger (Mt 23). We come to know God the Father personally through the work of the Holy Spirit (Rom 8:15, 16; Gal 4:6, 7), who enables us to know and approach him as our "Abba," dear Father. 60–61

34. What did Jesus expect of those who believed his message?
To be a follower of Jesus, it was necessary both to know what he said and to put it into practice. "Disciple" literally

means a student or follower. Jesus expected people to follow after him so they could be formed, taught, and trained in the ways of God and his reign. This meant that his disciples were to count nothing else on earth as important as following Jesus whether in happiness or sorrow, well-being or suffering (Mt 4:18–22; Lk 18:18–22). *61*

35. What does Jesus expect today of those who believe in him?
The same thing, discipleship. Being a Christian demands this same radical commitment. We are called to pick up our cross every day and follow him (Mk 8:34–38). Jesus Christ is not just a figure of the past or a theological problem but a living person who is calling each of us into a vital, intimate relationship of love with himself. Each one of us must choose to become his disciple, his follower. We are called to love Jesus Christ above all else. *61–62*

36. What about the salvation of those who do not know, believe in, or follow Jesus Christ?
Catholics do not claim to know the eternal destiny of any individual, but they do affirm certain things. First, we know that Jesus Christ is the only Savior (Acts 4:12). Second, the ordinary way for one to attain salvation is through faith, baptism into Christ and his church, and a life of discipleship, that is, a life of loving, faithful obedience to Jesus and his teaching (Mk 16:15–16). Third, in God's mercy it is possible for those who are not Christians to be saved through the grace of Jesus Christ. Certain biblical texts (Mt 25; Rom 2:12–16) indicate that some will be saved by Christ on account of their charity and through earnestly seeking God and striving to obey him while following the dictates of their own good consciences. Even then, it is not their charity or efforts that save them, but the mercy and grace of God that comes to the world in Jesus Christ. *62–63*

37. Can we assume that those who are not living as disciples as Jesus Christ will be saved?

No. It is possible that they may receive the grace of Christ in an extraordinary way, but we cannot presume this. Our commission as disciples of Jesus Christ is clear: to make disciples of all nations (Mt 28:19). We commend those who have not heard or accepted the message of Jesus Christ to the plan and mercy of God and continue to pray and work for their conversion to Christ. He alone is "the Way, the Truth, and the Life" (Jn 14:6; Acts 4:12). *64–65*

38. Who is called to be a disciple of Jesus Christ?

All people are called to be disciples. Jews, Gentiles, men, women, the rich and poor, the old and young, were all included as Jesus' disciples (Mt 8:10–11; 15:24; Lk 4:18; 19). His call is universal. It extends to all races, nations, peoples, and cultures (Gal 3:26–28). The key to discipleship is faith in Jesus Christ—faith that expresses itself in love, commitment, and obedience. As Catholics, we are called to carry on Jesus' mission of proclaiming and establishing the reign of God in this world by leading others to faith in and discipleship to Jesus Christ. *65–66*

39. Miracles, powerful teaching, seeing Jesus at work: is discipleship always so exciting?

Oftentimes it is, but discipleship always involves carrying the cross as Jesus did (Mk 8:34–35; Mt 16:24–25; Lk 9:23–24; Gal 6:14). In fact, Jesus rebuked those who sought "signs and wonders" (Jn 4:48). Scripture makes it clear that it is necessary to follow Jesus even when it means renouncing one's own preferences, opinions, comforts, and will—dying to oneself. Jesus did not live to please himself but to obey the will of his Father. The Father's will for the redemption of the human race was that his Son Jesus would suffer and die (Phil 2:8). The joy and fulfill-

ment of Christians is found, as Jesus found it, in doing the
will of God our Father. *66*

40. Why did the Son of God have to die?
Being God, he was not subject to death in his divine nature. He did not *need* to die. Rather he *chose* to die (Mt
26:53–54). He chose to accept and conquer death for the
sake of humanity (Heb 2:9–10; 7:27; 9:11–15; 1 Pt 3:18). His
death revealed the depth of God's love for us (Jn 15:13;
Rom 5:7–8). His death proved God's love for us and freed
us from the bondage of our sin. *66–67*

**41. What are some ways of understanding the meaning of
Jesus' death?**
Historically, there are many approaches to understanding
the saving value of Jesus' death including as a ransom, as
atonement or satisfaction, as a penal substitute, and as a
sacrifice. *67*

**42. What does it mean that Jesus' death was a ransom to
redeem sinners?**
Jesus' suffering and death may be looked at as a ransom,
the price that Jesus paid to redeem or free the human race
from its slavery to the devil (Mk 10:45; Is 52–53). His own
priceless life was given in exchange for the release of the
human race. The effect of Jesus' death was to reconcile the
human race with God (2 Cor 5:17–18). *67–68*

43. How is Jesus the atonement for our sins?
Mankind's sin is detestable and offensive to God. Jesus'
death may be looked upon as a free gift offered to God to
atone or make reparation for the sins of the human race.
Jesus' death makes satisfaction; it satisfies God's just requirement that sin should be punished or repaired. *68*

44. What is an example to help explain this concept?

Think of all the suffering resulting from a war: loss of life; destruction of property, of well-being, of peace; horror and disruption of families in all the nations affected by the war. How could anyone restore what even one single person lost due the sins that cause war? Human lives are irreplaceable; the financial costs to every nation involved is inconceivable. So much of what is destroyed is intangible, touching the realm of the human spirit. No one could atone or make satisfaction to the human persons affected by a single war, let alone make atonement to God. Yet Jesus Christ, through his suffering and death, has incomparably atoned or paid back to God for this and for every sin since the beginning and until the end of time (Rom 15:10–11).

45. What does "penal substitute" mean?

Jesus freely chose to accept, on behalf of the the whole human race, the death penalty resulting from sin; he substituted himself as a victim for each one of us (1 Pt 2:24). *68*

When ten prisoners were condemned to die in a starvation bunker during World War II, Maximilian Kolbe, a Franciscan priest who has been canonized as a saint, offered to take another man's place and die instead of him. This example typifies what Jesus Christ did for each of us.

46. Why is Jesus' death a sacrifice? What does it mean that he expiated our sins?

In the Old Covenant, the high priest would offer the flesh and blood of animals to God as a sacrifice to plead for the forgiveness of the people's sins. The Letter to the Hebrews portrays Jesus as the great High Priest who offers to God once for all his own body and blood for the forgiveness and redemption of the whole human race. A spotless lamb was the Jewish people's Passover sacrifice; Jesus is the spotless lamb, for he was without sin, our perfect sacrifice.

To expiate means to remove. Jesus removed, by his death, the sins of all. *68–69*

47. What does it mean to say that Jesus was raised from the dead?

No one actually witnessed the resurrection. Though the Gospel accounts vary, they all agree that the tomb in which Jesus had been buried was found empty with the entrance stone rolled away and that Jesus appeared alive to his followers. *70*

48. Why is the resurrection important?

The bodily resurrection of Jesus Christ from the dead is a central Christian belief, perhaps *the* central Christian belief. It formed the heart of the earliest proclamation of the gospel (Acts 2:22–36; 3:13–15; 4:10; 1 Cor 15:3–5). The hope of Christians hinges on the reality of the resurrection of Jesus (1 Cor 15:17–20, 32). The resurrection of Jesus is the act of God that reveals that death, sin, and Satan have been conquered. Therefore, Easter, the feast of Jesus' resurrection, is the most important holy day for Christians. *69–70*

49. Couldn't the disciples have seen a mere hallucination or meant "He is risen" as a figure of speech meaning that Jesus lived on in their hearts and minds?

Paul's First Letter to the Corinthians, written around A.D. 50, lists the witnesses who saw Jesus alive (including Paul himself) and even mentions that on one occasion five hundred brothers saw Jesus (1 Cor 15:6). Is it possible that all these people (including the apostles) were victims of the same hallucination? If we doubt the New Testament witnesses concerning this crucial fact, how can we believe anything else they have to say? Paul asserts that if Christ did not truly rise from the dead, our faith is in vain (1 Cor 15:17). *70*

50. What was Jesus' risen body like?

What his body was like surpassed the disciples' comprehension in some way (Jn 20:14; 21:12; Mt 28:17; Lk 24:16, 37–39). The Gospel accounts imply that Jesus' risen body was in some ways the same as the body that was buried in the tomb, but it was also different. His risen body was *not* just a resuscitation of the corpse that was buried, neither was it an entirely different body. We may best describe Jesus' body after the resurrection as a glorified, transfigured body or a "spiritual" body (1 Cor 15:42–44). 71

51. What will our own risen bodies be like?

Like the body of Jesus (1 Cor 15:49, 53–57; Phil 3:21). 71

52. What is the ascension of Jesus?

The ascension means that Jesus returned to his Father in heaven in his glorified body. Although he is the Second Person of God, Jesus forever retains this glorified human body. In Luke's account, this event occurred forty days after the resurrection, which we commemorate every Ascension Thursday, forty days after Easter. (Acts 1:1–11). 71–72

53. Since Jesus went to heaven does that mean he is no longer present to us?

No, not at all. Jesus no longer dwells on earth bodily nor appears in his glorified, risen body, but he is still present to us through the sacraments in his church (1 Cor 12:27), and by the Holy Spirit. He also dwells in our hearts through faith (Eph 3:17). 72

54. Why did the Holy Spirit come to us?

There are many dimensions to the Holy Spirit's mission among us. The most important reason the Holy Spirit comes to us is to give us living personal knowledge of God as Father, Son, and Holy Spirit. In other words, the Holy

Spirit reveals God to us and draws us into a relationship with him.

Another reason the Holy Spirit comes to us is to empower Christians to fulfill the "just requirement of the law" and to live the radical new commandment of love and the beatitudes that Jesus taught. The sending of the Holy Spirit fulfills Jesus' promise (Jn 14:16–17) and completes the establishment of the New Covenant. *73–74*

55. What is the New Covenant?
The New Covenant is a new life lived in Christ (Gal 2:19–21; Rom 6:4ff). It isn't a return to the relationship man enjoyed with God in Eden or the power to live out the covenant given at Mount Sinai. It is far more than that: it is a new relationship of sonship or daughterhood with God as our dear Father, through the merits of Jesus Christ.

56. Will Christ return again?
Jesus will come again according to Scripture (Acts 1:11; Heb 9:28; Dn 7:13–14; Rv 11:15). This is called the second coming of Christ or the *parousia*. Christians believe that Jesus will return in his glorified body and with all the unimaginable splendor of the king of the universe. "He will come again in glory to judge the living and the dead," as Christians profess in the Apostles' Creed. When he returns, the kingdom of God will be fully established, and his glorious kingship will be revealed. *75–76*

THREE

Church

1. Where did the term *church* originate? What does it mean?

The word *church* originated with the Jewish term *qahal* meaning an assembly or gathering. The Greek term *ekklesia*, which we translate into English as church, also means to assemble or "call forth" a people. The church, then, is the people of God of the New Covenant, the assembly of those whom God has called forth to be his people and to do his will. *77–78*

2. Does "church" refer to the building we go to or to the congregation of worshipers?

The New Testament uses the word *ekklesia* or church in two ways. It refers either to all of the believers in Jesus Christ, the universal church, or to the believers in a specific city or region, such as "the church in Galatia." These smaller groups saw themselves as branches or local units of the one universal church.

The New Testament never uses the word church (*ekklesia*) to refer to a building. However, we can refer to the church as a building, the "house of God," (Greek, *kyriake*) as long as we remember that its primary meaning is the "assembly of God's people." *78*

3. What is the nature of the church?

The church is a mystery which can only be understood through faith, like the mystery of the Trinity or of Jesus Christ. Used in this sense of the word, a mystery is not a puzzle to be solved, but a reality beyond whatever the most brilliant human mind can comprehend.

The church is also a sacrament, a sign of God's presence in the world and an instrument for bringing about the salvation and unity of mankind. There are many biblical images that reveal certain aspects of the church's nature: the church is the body of Christ and the bride of Christ, God's vineyard and field, a holy temple where the Spirit of God dwells, the new Israel, and the new Jerusalem, our mother. Each image helps us to understand a particular aspect of the nature of the church.

4. When did the church begin?

The church existed in God's mind before all time and was foreshadowed in Mary's "yes" to God and her perfect obedience to his plan. Jesus laid the foundation for the church during his public ministry by his preaching, healing, exorcism, selecting and training of the twelve apostles. He sealed the New Covenant between God and man by the shedding of his blood on Calvary. Yet the church was not fully completed or "born" until Jesus sent the Holy Spirit at Pentecost to empower, teach, and guide God's new people (Jn 16:7–15; Lk 24:49; Acts 1:12–14; 2). A car, for example, is complete as it leaves the assembly line, but it cannot run without fuel. The church was essentially complete at the time of Jesus' death and resurrection, but it could not accomplish its mission without the power of the Holy Spirit. *78–79*

5. What did it mean to be a member of the church for the earliest Christians?

Right from the beginning, it is clear that there were no

solitary Christians. Becoming a follower of Jesus through faith and baptism meant becoming part of his body, the church. Life in the church is a shared life in which we receive our beliefs from the elders (the apostles' teaching). We receive spiritual nourishment from the Eucharist (the breaking of the bread) and prayer (both personal and communal) and the study of God's Word in sacred Scripture. We also give and receive personal and material support (fellowship, or community, and sharing of possessions). These elements of the church's life, all found in Acts 2:41–47, have been evident and essential from its very beginning. *80*

6. This sounds like a family. Could you say that the church is God's family?
Exactly. Jesus revealed that God is our Father, and the members of the church are his adopted sons and daughters. We really are brothers and sisters of Jesus Christ and of one another in Christ. *80–81*

7. What is the "communion of the saints?"
All members of the church, whether living or dead, are related to each other as brothers and sisters in Jesus Christ and as sons and daughters of God our Father. We are in communion or fellowship with one another. This is true whether we are in the church here on earth (the church militant, still fighting the good fight of faith), fully united to God in heaven (the church triumphant), or being cleansed from any remaining bondage of sin in purgatory (the church suffering). *81*

8. Do Catholics worship the saints in heaven?
No, we do not worship the saints in heaven or pray to them as we pray to God, since worship or adoration is due to God alone. We honor or venerate these saints as examples of Christian virtue, imitate their faith, love, and

holiness, and ask them to pray for us. Christian tradition from the first centuries encourages this honor given to the saints and urges us to ask them to intercede for us to God. Nowhere does the Bible prohibit this approach to the saints. *82*

9. Why do we pray for the suffering souls in purgatory?
Catholics believe that God purifies the souls of those who die in the grace of God, but who have some unrepented sin or the effects of sin still remaining at the time of their death. This purging is experienced like fire (1 Cor 3:15) and is very painful. Therefore, Christians have had a long tradition of praying for those who have died, a practice which began among God's people in Old Testament times (2 Mac 12:41–46). We ask God's mercy on them and pray that any purification necessary for them to enter to heaven would soon be completed. *82–83*

10. Why is Mary called the "mother of the church"?
From the cross, Jesus told John, "Behold your mother," after he had told Mary, "Woman, behold your son" (Jn 19:26–27). The early Christians understood that here Jesus was giving Mary to all his disciples, represented by the beloved disciple John, to be their mother. In this sense, Mary is the mother of the church. Another way to look at this special relationship is that since Mary is the mother of Christ, she is also the mother of the body of Christ, the church. *84*

11. How is Mary a model or type of the church?
Mary is a model of the church because of her total obedience, her total "yes" to God. Mary is also the ideal model of discipleship because she faithfully followed and imitated her Son, Jesus Christ. She also possesses in fullness all the virtues that should characterize the church (Lk 1:28). *84*

12. What do the words "one, holy, catholic, and apostolic church" mean?

These are the primary characteristics or identifying marks of the church. We find them in the Nicene Creed which we profess every Sunday during the liturgy. Though they were formulated by two church councils to describe the church, they are biblical characteristics as well. 85

13. What does it mean that the church is "one"?

Jesus established only one people of the New Covenant, one church. Jesus prayed that the church be one even as he and the Father are one (Jn 17:21-23). The unity between the Father and the Son is the perfect model of our unity as followers of Jesus and members of his church.

Practically, this means that we hold a common faith, share in the same sacraments, show a mutual love for our fellow believers, and recognize and give allegiance to the same leaders and pastors, the pope, and bishops in communion with him. 85

14. How can the church be called "one" when there are so many divisions among Christians?

Catholics recognize that the division of the church violates the will of God. Today the ecumenical movement, inspired by the Holy Spirit, seeks to restore unity among all Christians. An impressive sign of the new ecumenical thrust by Catholics, especially accentuated at the Second Vatican Council, was the historic meeting between Pope Paul VI and the Orthodox Patriarch Athenagoras, in which they nullified all previous excommunications and actions taken against each other. 86

15. What is the ecumenical movement?

It is a movement, inspired by the grace of the Holy Spirit, that seeks the restoration of unity among all Christians. 86

16. Are the Jewish people part of the ecumenical movement?

No, by definition the ecumenical movement seeks unity among all those who believe in the Trinity and confess Jesus Christ as Lord and Savior. However, seeking unity with non-Christians, especially our Jewish brethren, is also an important concern and mission of the Catholic church. 87

17. How should Christians relate to the Jews?

The Catholic church vigorously condemns anti-Semitism—any bitterness, discrimination, or persecution directed against the Jewish people. We value the many Jewish elements that pervade our Catholic and Christian heritage. With love and deep respect, we continue to proclaim to God's people of the first covenant that God has a fuller plan in mind for them that they are always welcome to accept. 44

18. How are Catholics to approach other Christians to promote the restoration of unity?

There are several guidelines, but these are most important:

1. We must recognize that we bear a share of the blame for the division among Christians and ask the forgiveness of God and of our fellow Christians for this sin. We also forgive others for all offenses, past and present.
2. Our primary duty is to work for the renewal of the Catholic church, so that the life of its members may be a clearer witness to its teachings. Since we believe that the Catholic church possesses the fullness of Christian truth and life, we must express this truth and life in the way we live our Catholic faith.
3. Other Christians who are baptized and believe in the Trinity and in Jesus Christ as Lord and Savior are

viewed by Catholics as our "separated brothers and sisters," not heretics or schismatics.
4. We should state the teachings of the Catholic church clearly, fully, and non-defensively when speaking with other Christians. Without ignoring our differences, we can still join with others in working on common social concerns and in professing our common faith in Christ to the whole world. We need to remember that what unites us is greater than what divides us. *87–89*

19. What does the word *catholic* in the Nicene Creed mean?
It means "universal" or "all-embracing." Jesus Christ intended his church to embrace all people (1 Tm 2:4). All people are eligible to seek membership in the church, and the mission of the church has reached out to all races, nations, and cultures. It is in this sense that the Nicene Creed uses the word "catholic."

The name *Catholic* as a formal name for the church that Christ founded (the Catholic church) was used by Christian writers beginning in the second and third centuries. *89–90*

20. What does it mean that the church is "holy"?
Something is holy because it is chosen or set apart by God for his purposes and service (1 Pt 2:9). God has chosen and set apart the church to be his New Covenant people. That is why it is holy. The holiness of the church is also something that God is bringing progressively to completion or fulfillment in history, until it is finally perfected when Christ returns. The holiness of the church doesn't mean the sinlessness or perfection of its individual members. God himself guarantees the church's holiness; it doesn't depend on the righteousness or holiness of its individual human members. *91–92*

21. How is the church "apostolic"?

The church is built or founded on the apostles (Eph 2:20) because it announces and preserves the true teaching of the apostles and because the office or ministry of the apostles, established by and in Christ, is continued in unbroken succession to this day (1 Cor 12:28; Eph. 4:11). *93–94*

22. Who continued the teaching office and ministry of the apostles after they died?

The bishops (Greek: *episcopoi*) assumed the ministry and office of the apostles in the early church (1 Tm; 2 Tm; Ti). They were also the primary shepherds and leaders of the local churches. The bishops are the successors of the apostles: a body of men who carry out the Lord's commission to proclaim the gospel and lead the church in unity until the end of time. *94–95*

23. How does someone become a bishop today?

The pope appoints all the world's bishops, working through apostolic delegates and other means of consultation and discernment. Through episcopal consecration, the fullness of the priesthood of Jesus Christ is conferred upon a priest through the imposition of hands and words of consecration. This is how one becomes a bishop.

Bishops are enabled by the Holy Spirit to undertake Christ's own role as teacher, shepherd, and high priest in such a clear and visible way that they act in his person. This means that bishops have full apostolic authority in their own local churches or dioceses to guide and govern God's people in the name of Christ. Usually their jurisdiction is over a certain geographical area. *95–96*

24. What does "collegiality" mean?

The Second Vatican Council emphasized that the bishops are to see themselves and to function as fellow members of a college or body of bishops. Practically, this means that each bishop has a pastoral concern and care for the whole church as well as for his particular diocese or jurisdiction. One way collegiality is expressed is when the bishops meet together in synods or councils, where they pray and confer about God's direction for the church. *96*

25. Are the decisions they make at councils binding on the whole church?

Catholics believe that the Holy Spirit guides the church in a special way when the worldwide college of bishops, convened by and in union with the pope, meets together in an ecumenical council. The solemn doctrinal definitions of such councils are believed by Catholics to be infallibly true and therefore binding on the whole church. We firmly believe that God would not allow Satan to deceive the whole body of bishops. *96*

26. Are individual bishops infallible?

No. Individual bishops may err, but when the bishops united with the pope solemnly define a doctrine regarding of faith or morals that teaching is infallibly true. In that case, they assuredly fulfill Christ's promise that the Holy Spirit will guide the church into all truth (Jn 16:12–15). *96*

27. What is the hierarchy of the church?

The ordained offices of bishops, priests, and deacons comprise the hierarchy of the church. The pastoral epistles speak of bishops, elders or presbyters, and deacons as the leaders of the young Christian church. The bishop St. Ignatius of Antioch wrote a number of letters to various churches around A.D. 107–110 listing bishops, presbyters, and deacons as the leaders of the churches to which he wrote. This three-tiered structure of a bishop heading each local diocese assisted by priests and deacons was universally accepted in the church by the middle of the second century and has been preserved in the Catholic church to this day. *97–98*

28. What is the role of the pope in the hierarchy?

The chief representative or vicar of Jesus Christ and the spiritual head of the Roman Catholic church is the pope, the bishop of Rome. The pope is viewed as the successor to the specific apostle singled out by Jesus to be leader and shepherd of the whole church, St. Peter (Mt 16:18). *100–101*

29. How do we know that Jesus did single out Peter to have a special responsibility for the guidance and care of the church?

The biblical evidence for this is convincing: Matthew, Luke, and John's Gospels all strongly indicate that Peter was specifically set aside and commissioned by Jesus (Mt 16:18–19; Lk 22:31–32; Jn 10:14–18; 21:15–17). Peter did, in fact, emerge as the pre-eminent elder of the New Testament church (Acts 2:14–40; 10:46–48; Mk 8:29; Mt 18:21; Lk 9:20). *100–101*

30. Did Peter have a successor?

There is no word of Jesus that indicates that either Peter or the apostles were to be succeeded by others in their positions of authority and leadership. However, Jesus intended the church he founded to endure until he returned at the end of time, and the early Christians recognized the importance of having a leader in each church. Just as the bishops were raised up to serve within the local church, the universal church gradually came to see the value and the necessity of recognizing the special authority of one of the bishops—following Jesus' example of giving Peter a special leadership role among the apostles. The bishop of Rome was seen to have preeminence because of his direct link to the apostles, Peter and Paul. Both men were martyred in Rome and gave their final teachings there. Thus, the popes are considered by Catholics to be the successors of St. Peter. *101–103*

31. When did the title *pope* originate?
By the middle of the fourth century, the bishop of Rome was first called pope, "papa" or "father," a title that revealed his special care for the entire church. *102*

32. What is the doctrine of infalliblity?
The Catholic belief that the church cannot be led astray from the truth when it believes and formally defines a doctrine under the guidance of the Holy Spirit is called infallibility. It is based on the promises of Jesus to be with the church and to send the Holy Spirit to guide it into the fullness of truth and reveal the things to come (Jn 14:16; 16:13). *103*

33. In what ways is the church infallible?
First, the church as a whole is infallible when all the faithful throughout the world recognize and agree upon a truth in the sphere of faith and morals. Second, Christian doctrine can be stated infallibly by the bishops of the church when they, in union with the pope, formally define a doctrine concerning faith or morality. Third, Catholics believe that the pope, in specific circumstances, can speak with the gift of infallibility that Jesus Christ has given to his church. In each case, something is only known as infallibly true through the guidance of the Holy Spirit. Since infallibility is a gift of God, a charism, it is certainly possible for God to enable the person who holds the office of chief teacher, the pope, to speak infallibly on certain occasions, just as God inspired Peter to speak truth infallibly through revelation on at least two occasions (Mt 16:17; Acts 10:9–48). *103–104*

34. What is the doctrine of papal infallibility?

The First and Second Vatican Councils declare that the pope speaks infallibly when he proclaims by a definitive act some doctrine concerning faith or morals. The pope does not speak infallibly on every occasion. *103–104*

For example, papal encyclical letters such as John Paul II's *Redemptor Hominis* (Redeemer of Mankind) contain sure Christian truth, but they are not presented in the form of an infallible definition of Christian doctrine.

35. Papal infallibility was defined in 1870. Has the pope only been infallible in matters of faith and morals since then?

No. Though the doctrine of papal infallibility was only formally defined at the First Vatican Council, Catholics had long understood that the pope possessed this gift. The council merely defined more specifically when and how the pope was speaking with the charism of infallibility. *104*

36. Do we need to believe the pope's teaching if he is not speaking infallibly?

The Second Vatican Council teaches the Catholic faithful are to accept and adhere to the teaching of the pope with "a religious assent of soul" or a "religious submission of mind," even when he is not defining doctrine infallibly, because the pope is the chief earthly teacher of all Christians. *105*

37. How do the people of God participate in the church?

There are various ways that all members contribute to the mission and activity of the church, but each member participates most directly through the way of life God calls him or her to: through the ministerial priesthood, religious life, or the lay state of life.

38. What is the "religious life"?

This is a special classification of men and women in the Catholic church who have dedicated themselves to God in a solemn and permanent way through their profession of vows of poverty, chastity (or celibacy), and obedience. Most commit themselves to a particular community of men or women guided by a rule of life. There are religious orders for men who are priests or brothers and also for women who are sisters. Religious life is a great gift to the church and a sign of the life to come. They are a constant reminder to the whole church of the call to live for God alone. *106–107*

39. What is meant by the "lay state of life"?

The laity do not take vows, as the religious do, nor are they ordained to the ministerial priesthood. Rather they are called to live the gospel as a "leaven" for Christ in the midst of the secular world, as single or married people. Often their occupations are not directly related to the church. *107*

40. What is the lay person's ministry in the church?

The lay person is specifically sent to the world to extend the body of Christ and bring the influence of the church and gospel to bear upon the world's affairs, to order all things according to the will of God. They have been equipped for this apostolate by the gifts (charisms) and virtues of the Holy Spirit. The laity are to be active in service and leadership in the church as well, working in willing cooperation with the church's ordained pastors. In addition, they have their own areas of responsibility as lay people in their various fields of ministry and work. All lay people, for example, are called to evangelize: to call others to a personal knowledge of Christ to the best of their ability in the course of daily life. *107–108*

41. Are lay people called to a lesser degree of holiness in the kingdom of God than priests and vowed religious?
All people, regardless of their vocation, are equally called by God to the fullness of holiness or Christian perfection. Each person must pursue holiness and perfection in Christ according to his or her state in life and particular calling from the Lord. A married woman with small children, for example, will seek holiness in a different way from a cloistered contemplative nun. But both are equally called to holiness and equally able to attain it, though in different ways. The foundations of holiness: love of God and neighbor, prayer, the sacraments, and demonstrating the character of Christ, do not depend on one's vocation but upon one's willing and total response to God. *109–110*

42. Who will be saved and attain eternal life with God?
Eternal life or salvation is a free gift of God. Catholics believe that God can confer this gift of eternal life upon anyone, even those who do not belong to a Christian church. However, the Catholic church teaches that membership in the church is the normal or ordinary way to salvation. The *Dogmatic Constitution on the Church* of the Second Vatican Council states that the church is "necessary for salvation" because Jesus himself said that faith and baptism were necessary, and therefore he established the need for the church (no. 14). However, church membership alone is not sufficient for salvation. This same constitution teaches that even the baptized will not be saved unless they persevere in charity (Mt 22:37–40). *110–111*

43. Did Jesus teach that there was only one church?
Yes. Therefore he only established and founded one church (Eph 4:5). *111*

44. Where is that one church to be found today?
Catholics believe that the church of Jesus Christ truly ex-

ists (or subsists) in its fullness in the Catholic church, since its foundation can be traced directly back to Jesus and it is truly one, holy, catholic, and apostolic. Hence, it is correct for Catholics to say that they belong to the authentic church of Jesus Christ, which is governed by the successors of Peter and the other apostles. However, it is important to add that elements of the true church of Jesus Christ and the grace of salvation may be found outside the visible structure of the Catholic church. *111–112*

45. What does that mean for other Christian churches?
The teaching of the Catholic church is that although the Catholic church possesses and preserves the fullness (or fullest measure) of Christian truth and the means of salvation, other Christian churches and communities also possess some measure of truth and grace that can genuinely lead their members to salvation and impel them toward catholic unity. *112–113*

46. Is the Catholic church proud or narrow-minded in claiming that it alone possesses the fullness of Christian truth and the means of salvation?
No. This claim is based on a historical argument: that the Catholic church has preserved and faithfully handed on Christian truth and practice down through the centuries in spite of the personal sinfulness of its members and its corporate weakness and failings. Indeed, she is assured by Christ himself that "the powers of death shall not prevail against it" (Mt 16:18). Second, the same documents that make these statements readily admit that the Catholic church is not perfect but is a holy pilgrim people always needing to repent and to receive God's mercy and grace. Whatever goodness or truth there is present in the Catholic church is entirely due to God. *114*

47. Are we saved by the church or are we saved by Jesus Christ?

Salvation is totally based on the grace of Jesus Christ. Ultimately the church doesn't save us, but it does provide the means through which we can encounter Jesus and enter into his life most fully. God saves us in the person of Jesus Christ, normally in and through the chosen instrument of his church. *115*

48. Is it enough just to go to church to be saved?

No. It is up to each individual to take advantage of the various means the church offers of coming to know, love, and follow Jesus. Faith in Christ means much more than going to church. The Catholic church possesses an abundant fullness of the means of salvation through which our faith is expressed and lived out. These means include the sacraments, prayer, worship, works of mercy, and the intercession of Mary and the saints, for example. Catholics who fail to take advantage of these and do not persevere in charity will be judged more severely and possibly even forfeit the eternal life that God is offering them through the church (Lk 12:48). *115–116*

49. Is there anything we can learn or appreciate in other Christian churches?

Certainly. Though the Catholic church alone possesses the fullness of Christian truth and the means of sanctification (saving grace), other Christian churches also possess many elements of grace and truth. What Catholics have in common with other Christians is far greater than what divides us. The Decree on Ecumenism of the Second Vatican Council lists the most important similarities (and differences) between the Catholic church and the Eastern (mainly Orthodox) Christian churches (nos. 14–18), and the Catholic church and the separated churches and ecclesial communities in the West (nos. 19–20).

Catholics believe that nothing genuinely Christian is foreign to the Catholic church, and so we should be ready to appreciate and be inspired by the genuinely Christian heritage and aspects of other Christian churches, as they should be ready to learn and benefit from our Catholic heritage. *115*

FOUR

How God Reveals Himself

1. How can Christians claim to know with certainty things about God and his will for the human race?
Christians affirm that God's existence should be evident from observing the beauty and order of the universe which we call natural revelation (Ps 19:1; Rom 1:19–20). Christians also believe that God offers the human race a more accurate and complete knowledge of himself and his will through what theology calls supernatural or divine revelation. *117–118*

2. What comprises supernatural revelation?
The faith of Christians and Jews is based on the belief that God acts in unique and specific ways in human history and that he also speaks to humanity in various ways. In other words, God reveals himself to us through words and deeds. For example, through the retelling of the Exodus from Egypt, each generation came to know God's saving power. Both the event and the retelling of the story reveal God's love and will to save his people. *118*

3. What is the ultimate source of revelation?
The Catholic church has always emphasized that the ulti-

mate source of revelation is not the Bible, nor a tradition, nor the Magisterium (the teaching office of the pope and bishops), but is God himself as he has revealed himself most fully in Christ and continues to speak to us in the person of the Holy Spirit. In other words, God is the *source* of revelation, while the church's teaching and Scripture are vehicles or means used by God to communicate his revelation of himself to us. *119*

4. What does the Holy Spirit reveal to God's people?
A primary work of the Holy Spirit is to testify to Jesus Christ, who is the climax of God's revelation of himself to humanity (Jn 14:6). *119*

5. What does "public revelation" mean?
Those truths which God has made known, particularly contained in sacred Scriptures, for belief by all peoples for all time is public revelation. According to Catholic tradition, the period of public revelation ended with the death of the last apostles. This means that God will send no new savior, nor will there be any further revelation of God bearing the same authority or significance as his revelation in and through Jesus Christ. This public revelation provides for us the knowledge that can lead to salvation (1 Tm 6:14; Ti 2:13). *119–120*

6. What about other religions that claim that God has revealed another way in addition or apart from sacred Scriptures?
No other revelation is valid if it contradicts the good news received through the apostles and the traditions that they have passed on (Gal 1:8; 2 Thes 2:15). This is why Catholics do not accept as valid such "revelations" as the Book of Mormon or the teachings of Rev. Sun Myung Moon of the Unification Church. *120*

7. How do we know what is the true revelation of God?
The Catholic church teaches that the normative revelation of God, for all times and situations, comes to us from the Holy Spirit through two channels: sacred Scripture and sacred tradition. Both together make up God's revealed word. *120*

8. What is meant by "tradition"?
"Things handed on" or "that which is handed on" is the literal meaning of the word tradition. Many aspects of Christian life, worship, and belief coming from the time of the apostles were not written in the Bible. They were handed on by the apostles and their successors as essential parts of the life of the early church. For example, the order of the Mass—the Liturgy of the Word followed by the Liturgy of the Eucharist, including the prayers, numbers of readings and so forth—is not clearly found in Scripture. But it has been part of the church's life since the first two centuries. *121*

9. What is included in tradition?
Sacred tradition, sometimes called apostolic tradition or the Tradition, includes every aspect of God's revelation outside of the Bible that God intends to be believed and followed by the whole church in every age. Some aspects of sacred tradition pass on to us the fullest way to worship God in the church or the proper way to honor the angels and the saints, including Mary, the Mother of God. Other aspects of sacred tradition present God's will about how we are to live (the moral life), which is not always explicitly or fully spelled out in the Bible. Another role of tradition is to safeguard the true meaning of the sacred Scripture by presenting the church's authoritative interpretation of certain passages of the Bible. *121–122*

10. But doesn't following sacred tradition detract from the importance of the Bible?

To the contrary, Catholics express their great respect for the Bible by acknowledging that we often must rely on sacred tradition to preserve the true meaning of the Bible. No element of sacred tradition can contradict the teaching of the Bible since both are expressions of the one truth of God. Nowhere does the Bible teach that Scripture *alone* is inspired by God. Furthermore, certain themes which are only mentioned or implied in the Bible often are presented in greater fullness and depth through sacred tradition. An example of this is the Catholic beliefs about Mary's immaculate conception and assumption into heaven which are not explicitly stated in the Bible but which flow out of and deepen the biblical teaching about Mary. 122

11. Are all traditions within the church part of the divine revelation that Catholics refer to as sacred tradition?

No. There are many human traditions that are part of the church's tradition that are subject to change. These are either human customs, or they may be part of God's will and intention for the church for a particular situation or period of time in the life of God's people, but not for all time and every situation. For example, for many years priests celebrated Mass facing away from the people. Now the priest faces the people. This is an example of a tradition that can change to meet the needs of God's people. However, bread and wine must be used for the consecration and not beer and pretzels. Since a sacrament is a sacred, visible sign, you cannot arbitrarily change the elements or signs used by Jesus himself without changing the reality of the sacrament. 123

12. Where can we find the whole sacred tradition written down?

There is no single volume that contains all of what the

Catholic church considers sacred tradition, since this tradition includes much of the life of God's people, such as ways of worship, devotion, moral teaching and wisdom, and the interpretation and practical application of the Bible. Part of sacred tradition can be found in books that summarize the official teachings of ecumenical councils and popes of the Catholic church. These teachings are formal definitions of Catholic belief and practice that have been made by the teaching office or Magisterium of the Catholic church over the centuries. *123–124*

13. What does the "teaching office" (Magisterium) mean? Is it a department of the Vatican?

No. It is not a place like the principal's office or a group of people who decide what the church will teach. Rather, it is a task and a duty of the bishops united with the pope to authentically interpret the Word of God (found in sacred Scripture and sacred tradition), through the authority given to them by Jesus Christ.

14. What is "sacred Scripture?"

Sacred Scripture or the Bible is the record of God's revelation to the Hebrew people under the Old Covenant, known as the Old Testament, and also the record of revelation under the New Covenant or the New Testament. It is sacred because it is divinely inspired by the Holy Spirit (2 Tm 3:16, 17). *124*

15. Is the Old Testament unimportant or disposable because it has been surpassed by the New Testament?

The Catholic church has always valued and urged the study of the Old Testament, even though some elements of it (such as dietary laws and other ritual observances) have been surpassed or rendered unnecessary, based on Jesus' teaching and example. The Old Testament is part of our history and leads to a fuller understanding of God and his ways. Many of the figures and events of the Old Testament foreshadow the coming of Christ and the fullness of God's work among us in the church. It is an essential part of God's revealed truth for all Christians and has a value in and of itself for us. *125–126; 44–45*

16. Why do Catholics and Protestants have a different list of inspired writings in the Old Testament?
The writings included in the ancient Greek version of the Hebrew Scriptures are considered, by Catholics, to be divinely inspired. This version, known as the Septuagint, was used in the early church. There are forty-six writings of the Old Testament recognized by the Catholic church. Protestants accept only the writings found in an earlier Hebrew version of the Old Testament. *126*

17. How did the New Testament come into being?
During the first two centuries of the early church, various letters and Gospels circulated among the local churches that were purportedly written by the apostles and testified accurately to the apostles' faith in Jesus. However, some accounts (such as the Gospel of Thomas and others) appeared to many Christians to be evidently unreliable or untrue, so the church questioned whether all the letters that were passed around were really genuine. By the fifth century, the bishops of the church reached a general agreement about which letters and Gospels were truly inspired by God. This was the birth of the New Testament substantially as we know it today. *127–128*

18. How did those bishops know which Gospels and letters were true and which weren't?
As these books were read within the church the bishops prayerfully discerned their authenticity and oftentimes discussed this subject with other bishops in the region. It is the bishops' task to authentically proclaim and interpret

the Bible through the guidance of the Holy Spirit. This charism enabled the bishops to accurately discern the matter. Over time, the bishops increasingly agreed upon which ones were truly in harmony with the traditions they had received from the apostles. The Catholic church sees this as a fulfillment of Jesus' promise that the Holy Spirit would guide the church to recognize the teachings and writings that he had inspired. *128–129*

19. What does it mean that the Bible or a particular book of the Bible is inspired by God?

Inspired literally means "God-breathed." To say that the Bible has God as its author emphasizes that it is the Word of God and that it is a gift to the church. It doesn't mean that the human authors were mere transcribers for what God was dictating. They made use of their talents and strengths and their limitations in writing. For example, the Gospel of John is written in flawless Greek, while the Epistles of the apostle Peter are full of grammatical errors. Yet both are equally inspired by God.

To be inspired means that everything, and only those things, that God wanted to be consigned to writing were written by the human authors using their own talents and ways of speaking in relating the truth. *129–130*

20. Does the human dimension matter in understanding Scripture?

Yes. Because the Scriptures are "the words of God in the words of men," what the human authors had in mind, what they meant to write, is of utmost importance *in order* to understand what God wished to tell us. *130–131*

21. Can we know today what the authors of Scripture meant so long ago?

The Catholic church, since 1943, has given positive encouragement to biblical scholars to use modern methods of biblical criticism in order to understand more fully the human dimension and the cultural context for the writings of Scripture. Scholars determine what literary forms the sacred writers used, their customary and characteristic styles of approach, speech, and narrative, and the conventions that prevailed in the biblical author's world. *131*

22. Does this mean we cannot understand Scripture at all unless we are biblical scholars?
No. The findings of scholars, no matter how scientifically determined, are not enough in themselves to determine the authentic meaning of God's Word. The Bible must be approached with faith and prayer if it is to be correctly understood. The writings of the saints and the fathers of the church also need to be considered as well as modern research in determining the Bible's meaning. The Magisterium of the Catholic church has the final authority to interpret correctly the meaning of the sacred Scripture. *131*

23. Can you understand one passage of Scripture apart from the rest of the Bible?
Individual passages cannot be isolated from the overall message of Scripture and used as a weapon against other passages if they are to be interpreted correctly. In addition, the living tradition of the church must be taken into account. *131–132*

24. If the human authors were fallible, how can sacred Scripture be without error?
There are different understandings of the inerrancy of the Bible among Christians. Some Christians generally believe that everything stated by the Bible is literally true and that this truth is usually readily understandable to today's reader without the use of modern methods of biblical scholarship. The Second Vatican Council specifically teaches that God has preserved the Bible from error in truth per-

taining to our salvation; that is, in such matters as faith in God and morality. The Bible infallibly reveals how we are to relate to God and to each other in this world in order to fulfill God's plan and attain eternal salvation. There may be other truths contained in the Bible, but the Catholic church believes that only these truths pertaining to human salvation are without error—as a result of God's inspiration of the sacred Scripture. *132–135*

25. Is there an official understanding for every verse in the Bible?

No. Generally, the church officially limits the interpretation of a particular passage to times when it has been used to condemn a heretical teaching, such as when a biblical passage is used in order to protect the true faith. Consequently, it has been necessary to interpret very few passages officially. This leaves room for the contributions of the fathers of the church, saints, biblical scholars, and others who prayerfully reflect on the meaning of the Scriptures. *136*

26. Is human reason alone enough to interpret the Bible accurately?

No. The church has stressed that faith and the tradition of the church are necessary so that reason can exercise its proper role in understanding the Bible. The destructive effect of rationalism in interpreting the Bible cannot be underestimated. Human reason is not above the Word of God, but it is meant to serve it. *136–138*

27. Who determines the true meaning of Scripture, biblical scholars or the bishops?

The Catholic church teaches that God guides the universal college of the bishops of the church in discerning the true meaning of the Scriptures. That is, they cannot teach error whenever they meet together in an ecumenical or world-wide council and officially interpret a disputed passage of Scripture—or when they universally agree, even without formally meeting, on the meaning of a biblical text, or condemn an erroneous interpretation. Bishops benefit from the research and study of theologians and Scripture scholars. The pope, as the chief teacher in the church, possesses a special gift of God enabling him to proclaim and interpret the Scripture correctly. All Catholics are called to loyalty to the Catholic church's teaching office in case of any disputed interpretation. *137–138*

28. Does this mean the Magisterium is superior to Scripture?

No, the teaching office of the church is not more important or essential than Scripture. In fact, the Catholic Magisterium is to serve and defend the Word of God. Catholics today believe that their understanding of the relationship between the Bible, tradition, and church authority is the same as that which developed in the early church. These three elements are so linked and joined together that one cannot stand without the others, as with the three legs of a tripod. All three are equally needed. *139–140*

29. What is "private revelation"?

There are certain truths that God reveals through the Holy Spirit that either are not intended for the entire church or are not intended to be truths relevant for all times in the church's life. These are private revelations and include such things as words spoken through the gift of prophecy; messages from God spoken to an individual or a group through angels, saints, or Mary the Mother of God; visions, dreams, or voices that present a word from God to a person or persons; or even a word or appearance of Jesus Christ himself. *140*

30. How do we know if the message or vision is really from God?
The Catholic church insists that such private revelations must be discerned or tested carefully to insure that they are truly from God, lest some people be deceived. One important test is that no private revelation can contradict or disagree with public revelation, what God has revealed through the Bible or authentic Christian tradition. Genuine private revelation always complements and supports God's public revelation to his people. *140–141*

31. Do Catholics have to believe in a private revelation even if the church has no objection to its content?
No, because it is not part of the foundational public revelation to the people of God. All that is necessary for our salvation has already been revealed. However, God often has an important purpose in presenting a special private revelation, perhaps to awaken the church to a part of public revelation that he desires his people to act upon, or to call attention to his work and plan during a particular time in human history. *141*

32. If God still speaks to his people today, does he still perform mighty acts, like the miracles in Scripture?
Yes. Miracles, healings, exorcisms, and other mighty works are done in the name of Jesus and by his power. This should not surprise us, for Jesus told his disciples that they would perform even greater works than his (Jn 14:12). *141*

33. Has the Catholic church ever prohibited its members from reading the Bible?
Because the meaning of the Bible was being disputed and misinterpreted by some at the time of the Protestant Reformation, lay Catholics needed special permission from the bishop to read the Bible in their native tongue. Reading

the Latin Vulgate, the official Catholic Bible, was never prohibited. This was done to protect Catholics from inaccurate translations and from misinterpreting the Bible. Catholics still heard the Scriptures read and explained at Mass and in other contexts by the clergy, just as they always had. Today all restrictions have been lifted, and daily reading and study of the Bible is strongly encouraged by the church. *143–144*

34. How can Catholics better come to know God and his revealed Word?
1. Reading and studying the Bible (2 Tm 3:16, 17).
2. Studying teachings of past councils and popes.
3. Hearing the teaching of our present pope and bishops. *143–145*

FIVE

The Sacraments

1. How do Catholics approach God in worship?
Catholics approach God, as Jesus intended, both in personal prayer and in communal worship. The center of Catholic communal worship is our sacramental life, especially the Eucharist. *149*

2. How did Jesus approach God in worship?
Jesus taught his followers to address God as "Abba," or "Dear Father," which means coming to God with great affection and intimacy, as well as awe and respect. His intimacy with the Father never detracted from the respect and reverence that Jesus showed to his heavenly Father, nor diverted him from the desire to do the Father's will perfectly as the guiding principle of his life. The "Our Father" (Mt 6:9–13) sums up the characteristic elements of Jesus' prayer: reverence, joy, thanksgiving, perseverance, and petition. *149*

3. Why do Catholics value the sacraments so highly?
The major reason is that Catholics believe that God himself has given sacraments to the church to be privileged channels of his grace, his life, and his power. *149*

4. Where do the sacraments come from?
Catholics believe that all of the sacraments are based on

some important aspect of Jesus' life, teaching, and ministry. Jesus instituted some sacraments through an explicit
word or command, others through his example or teaching. Through the sacraments, Jesus continues to remain
with and minister to us "to the close of the age" (Mt 28:20).
150

5. What is a sacrament?
The word *sacrament*, comes from a Latin translation of the
Greek "mysterion" or "mystery" (Eph 1:9ff). They are
visible, tangible, effective signs through which God approaches us, enters into our lives, and draws us to himself
through his grace. The church and individual sacraments
are a continuation or an extension of the mission and ministry of Jesus and his incarnation. In Jesus, the Word of
God became man so that he could approach us, and we
approach him in a way that is perfectly suited to our bodily
human nature. *150–152*

6. What is the greatest sacrament of all?
Jesus Christ is the ultimate visible sign of God's presence
among us. Jesus is God himself, the Word of God who
lived among us as a human person. In Jesus, the fullness
of God's grace and love came into the world (Jn 1:16–17; 1
Jn 1:1–2). *150*

7. Can the church be called a sacrament?
Yes. Jesus left a visible body of faithful believers, his
church, to continue his presence in the world until the end
of time. The church is a sign and an instrument of communion with God and of unity among all peoples. Through
the church, subsequent generations of people have come
into contact with Jesus Christ and have believed in him.
The church makes Christ present through its preaching,
its actions, and through the particular saving sacraments.
151

8. How many sacraments are there in the Catholic church?
Seven: baptism, confirmation, Eucharist, reconciliation or penance, anointing of the sick, holy orders, and marriage.

9. What is the nature of the sacraments?
Sacraments have a twofold nature. First, they are signs that point to the presence of God among his people; second, they are also efficacious signs, that is, they bring about or effect what they signify. For example, when the child is immersed, or water is poured over his or her head, in conjunction with the words of baptism, the child really is baptized. *152*

10. Do you have to believe in the sacraments for them to be effective?
Christ is truly present and at work in any sacrament of the church which is celebrated properly by a valid minister. However, to obtain the full benefits and grace that God wishes to confer through the sacraments, it is important that we come to them with the proper dispositions or attitudes of heart and mind. Faith (believing in God and his work through the sacrament) and also reverence before the mystery of God and his presence in the sacrament should be our attitude when we approach any sacrament. *152*

11. Do we "make" God come and help us when we celebrate the sacraments?
Any interpretation of the sacraments as magic—conjuring up God or controlling God—is false. It is God who chooses to be present and to grant his graces and blessings through the sacraments, out of his infinite love and mercy. *152*

12. What makes up a sacrament?
First there is an outward, visible sign or action—such as water, the laying on of hands, or other visible public acts.

Second, the sacrament involves the proclamation of God's Word, announcing what God is doing in the particular sacrament. Third, the sacrament must be carried out by the appropriate minister of the church. In baptism, the sign would be the threefold immersion or pouring of water, and the words of baptism, "I baptize you in the Name of the Father, and the Son, and the Holy Spirit." This rite is usually performed by a priest, though in special circumstances any person could baptize. *152–153*

13. Can any Christian administer a sacrament?
Normally, the sacraments are administered by those in the church who have been formally set apart to represent Christ and to carry on his ministry, the bishops and priests and sometimes the deacon. *153*

14. If one doesn't feel anything or feel any different when receiving the sacraments, are they still effective?
Yes. Grace, God's life, is not something that can be accurately detected or measured by human experience or feelings. Catholics recognize the sacraments because we *believe* that they have been instituted by Jesus Christ, through his word or example, as a primary means of receiving his life and grace, not because we necessarily feel different when we receive them. They cannot be evaluated on the basis of experience, but they do have power. However, our awareness of God's presence in the sacraments can grow over the course of time. *154–155*

Baptism

15. What is the purpose of baptism?
Through baptism, Christians are delivered from original sin and darkness and made God's sons and daughters, members of his holy people. *155*

16. How did baptism become a sacrament?
Jesus directly instituted baptism by his command to his
followers:

> "Go, therefore and make disciples of all nations, baptiz-
> ing them in the name of the Father and of the Son and of
> the Holy Spirit . . ." (Mt 28:19)

In Mark 16:15–16 and John 3:5 the necessity of baptism
is also affirmed. *155–156*

17. What are the other effects of baptism?
Other major spiritual effects of baptism are: the forgiveness of sins, receiving the Holy Spirit, and entrance into
the fellowship of the church, as well as becoming a son or
daughter of God. *157*

18. How is someone baptized?
The basic form or rite of baptism is to pour water over a
person's head three times (or immerse the person in water
three times) while saying: "(Name), I baptize you in the
Name of the Father, and of the Son, and of the Holy
Spirit." *158*

**19. Can a lay person baptize someone in the case of an
emergency?**
Yes. Any Christian (or even a non-Christian) can administer baptism in the case of an emergency if they have the
intention of baptizing according to the belief of the Catholic church and use this basic rite. *158*

20. Why does the Catholic church baptize infants?
Since baptism brings salvation and seals membership in
God's family, the church, Catholics have long accepted the
practice of baptizing infants and children. Jesus himself
said to let the little children come to him (Mk 10:14). St.

Augustine of Hippo, a father of the church, was among many leaders of the early church who proclaimed the necessity of infant baptism for the salvation of infants and children. There are some biblical texts as well that may indicate infant baptism was practiced even in the primitive church—although it did not become common until the fifth century, since most of those baptized before then were adult converts. (Acts 2:39; 1 Cor 1:16; Acts 11:13b–14; 10:48a; 16:15, 33; 18:8). *158*

21. How can an infant or child be baptized or saved without a personal and mature faith in God?

Jesus never refused to bless or heal anyone on account of their age. Infant baptism reminds us that we cannot earn or merit salvation, even through our faith. Faith only enables us to receive or accept God's free gift of life in Jesus Christ. *159*

22. What role do the parents and godparents play in infant baptism?

The parents and godparents, as well as the witnessing church community, believe in God and accept his gift of new life on behalf of the child when he or she is baptized. This faith of the church is present and sufficient when an infant is baptized. *159*

23. Is it necessary for the parents or godparents to truly believe that God desires to give new life in baptism?

Yes. The Catholic church teaches that presenting a child to be baptized requires a commitment on the part of the parent or guardian to raise the child in an environment where he or she can grow in the Catholic faith. This will prepare the child to make a personal faith commitment to Jesus Christ upon reaching maturity. *160*

24. Can someone be rebaptized?
No. Rebaptism implies that God's work of salvation was ineffective the first time. The Catholic church believes that baptism imparts a permanent mark or character that sets the person apart in God's eyes as being one of his people, even if the person sins seriously or stops practicing the faith. *160*

25. How does someone return to the church if they have fallen away?
Any baptized Catholic who desires to return to the church should simply repent and seek forgiveness in the sacrament of reconciliation in order to renew and restore the grace first received at baptism. *160*

Confirmation

26. What is the purpose of confirmation?
The sacrament of confirmation is the bestowal, through prayer and anointing, of a fuller empowerment of the baptized person by the Holy Spirit so he or she may lead a fuller Christian life. One could say that baptism empowers us to be saved, and confirmation empowers us to live as bold witnesses to Christ in the world, carrying on his mission and ministry. *161*

27. Does the Bible speak about confirmation?
Yes, though it does not use this specific term. The Acts of the Apostles and the Gospel of John record certain sendings of the Holy Spirit distinct from baptism (Acts 2; 8:15–17; 19:6; Jn 20:22). *161*

28. How is the sacrament of confirmation conferred?
From early times, the bishops of the church have prayed with baptized Christians using the laying on of hands and

anointing with oil (to symbolize strengthening), asking God to send the Holy Spirit in fullness upon them. *161*

29. How can someone tell if the Holy Spirit has come more deeply in their life at confirmation?
Regardless of whether there are any outward signs or manifestations of the Spirit's coming, Catholics rely on Jesus' promise and know in faith that God grants through confirmation the gift of the Spirit that he so desires to give. *162*

30. Why do Catholics need a second prayer and anointing for the Holy Spirit to come into their life after baptism? Isn't baptism sufficient?
Baptism does fully initiate a person into the life of Christ and the church, but there is need for more grace and power (Acts 2:1–15). *162*

31. What effect does confirmation have in a Christian?
Confirmation changes a person in so profound a way that it can be received only once. God confers a new character, marks a person as his witness in a way that can never be erased. *162*

32. Why does a candidate for confirmation pick a sponsor?
To show the significance of the event, a sponsor is chosen as a support in this new dimension of the person's Christian life. The person also chooses a new name, the name of a saint who will support him or her in prayer. *162*

33. When should a person be confirmed?
There have been different views on this throughout the history of the church. Once it was administered with baptism and the Eucharist, but now the Roman Catholic church administers confirmation to older children, adolescents, and adults. The ability to make a mature choice, to

fully respond to God's graces, and to take on the responsibilities of confirmation is important in determining a candidate's readiness for the sacrament. *163*

Eucharist

34. What is the Eucharist?
Eucharist means "thanksgiving" in Greek. By the second century, Christians were using the word eucharist to designate their coming together to commemorate and reenact the Lord's Last Supper. *167*

35. How do Catholics understand the words of Jesus, "This is my body" (Mk 14:22) and "This is my blood . . ." (Mk 14:24)?
Catholic Christians understand these words in light of the commentary on them given in the Gospel of John (see John 6) and Paul's letters and the testimony of early Christians, namely, that the bread and wine consecrated in the Eucharist truly become the body and blood of Jesus. *165*

36. What do Catholics mean when they speak of the "real presence?"
Even though the outward appearance of the bread and wine do not change, Catholics accept in faith that the inner reality or essence of the bread and wine is transformed into the body and blood of Jesus. This is called "transubstantiation." *166–167*

37. Do Catholics worship bread and wine?
No. They worship Jesus Christ whom they discern by faith to be present "body and blood, soul and divinity" under the appearance of bread and wine. *167*

38. What does the Eucharist mean?
There are many ways of understanding the Eucharist be-

cause it is the realization and the summation of the entire Christian mystery of salvation. We can see the Eucharist as a covenant, as a memorial, as thanksgiving and sacrifice, as a communion, as nourishment, and as a work of the Holy Spirit anticipating the age to come. *168–171*

39. How is the Eucharist seen as a covenant?

A covenant is a solemn agreement commiting two parties. Moses sealed the covenant on Mount Sinai with the blood of sacrificial animals. The blood that sealed the new and final covenant of God with humanity is the blood of Jesus, the Son of God (Lk 22:20; Heb 9:11–28; 10:19–31). *168*

40. What does it mean that the Eucharist is a memorial?

The Eucharist is a *anamnesis*, a remembrance or memorial of what Jesus did at the Last Supper and of his whole life and ministry.

41. Does memorial mean remembering it mentally, like any another memory?

No. The biblical concept of memorial meant making something from the past actually present once more. Catholic Christians understand the Eucharist as memorial to mean that the reality of Jesus' body and blood is truly made present in the sacrament, under the appearances of bread and wine (Lk 22:19; 1 Cor 11:24, 25). *168*

42. How is the Eucharist a thanksgiving and a sacrifice?

The concepts of thanksgiving and sacrifice are closely connected. The sacrifice most pleasing to God is the offering of our entire being to him in thanksgiving and praise (Ps 40). Jesus himself offered the most perfect thanksgiving to God by offering his life as a sacrifice (Heb 10:10, 12, 14) to atone for the sins of humanity. *169*

43. Is Jesus sacrificed again every time the Eucharist is celebrated?

No. Catholics believe that in the Mass, Christ's one sacrifice on Calvary is represented (made present once again) or perpetuated. Christ's death on the cross is both an historical and a transhistorical event. Through God's love and mercy, in the Sacrament of the Eucharist, the one sacrifice of Jesus on Calvary is as real and powerful today as it was nearly two thousand years ago. *169*

44. What does it mean that the Eucharist is a communion?

In the Eucharist, we reaffirm our covenant relationship with God, sealed by the blood of Jesus. We come into communion with God and with one another as members of Christ's body, the church. *169*

45. When shouldn't we receive the Eucharist?

If any Catholic has broken the covenant with God through serious sin, he must seek forgiveness and be reconciled with God through the sacrament of reconciliation or penance before receiving the Lord's body and blood. Second, since participation in the Eucharist expresses our unity in Christ, any serious division between individual Christians should be settled before approaching the altar (Mt 5:23–24). *169–170*

46. Why doesn't the Catholic church allow *intercommunion*?

For Catholics, the Eucharist is the highest, most primary sign of the reality of our communion with God and our unity with one another. If there is serious disagreement among Christians that results in division into different denominations or churches, the Catholic church believes that reconciliation must first occur before we can receive communion together, except under special circumstances that are designated for Catholics by the local bishop. *170*

47. How does the Eucharist feed us?
Jesus teaches us that his body and blood are the spiritual
nourishment of our lives (Jn 6:32, 35, 54, 55). We receive
spiritual life and nourishment for our daily Christian life
when we approach the Eucharist in faith (1 Cor 11:27–29).
170–171

**48. In what way is the Eucharist a work of the Holy
Spirit?**
The Holy Spirit leads Christians to the Eucharist and enables them to recognize Jesus Christ as truly present there.
The church calls upon the Holy Spirit in the eucharistic
prayer to bless the bread and wine and the community
gathered together so that the elements will truly become
the body and blood of Christ and those assembled,
Christ's community. *171*

49. How does the Eucharist anticipate the age to come?
The Holy Spirit points toward the future when the sacramental presence of Christ will be replaced by seeing him
face to face (1 Cor 11:26). The Holy Spirit stirs up in the
hearts of believers the reality of the eucharistic response:
"Christ has died! Christ has risen! Christ will come again!"
171

Sacrament of Reconciliation

50. What is the sacrament of reconciliation?
Often called penance or confession, this sacrament is the
means through which God forgives sins committed after
baptism.

51. What is the origin of this sacrament?
Jesus' entire ministry was focused on reconciling humanity to God and to one another (Mk 2:7; Lk 7:49; 23:34; Jn
8:1–11; 21:15–19). He conferred special authority to forgive

sins in God's name upon the apostles (Mt 16:18, 19; 18:18; Jn 20:22–23). This is the origin of the sacrament of reconciliation. *172*

52. What is absolution?

The church's official act of forgiveness is called absolution. Normally, it is given after the private confession of one's sins to a priest or bishop. In special circumstances, a bishop may allow a communal absolution to be given to a group receiving the sacrament of reconciliation together. *173–174*

53. Why don't Catholics confess their sins only to God instead of to another human being?

It is good to seek God's forgiveness immediately through prayer when we sin. When Catholics participate in the sacrament of reconciliation, they are expressing their repentance and sorrow for sin to God and seeking to be reconciled to him. The priest acts as a special representative of Christ by virtue of his ordination, and exercises the authority of Christ to forgive sins and reconcile the sinner with God. *173–174*

Besides, there is a further healing that occurs by confessing sins to another human being, a humbling and honest cleansing occurs. Scripture admonishes, "Hence, declare your sins to one another, and pray for one another, that you may find healing" (Jas 5:16). *174*

54. Who forgives sins, the priest or Jesus Christ?

It is not the priest who grants forgiveness of sins, but God who uses the priest as an instrument and a sign of his mercy. The priest acts *in persona Christi*, "in the person of Christ," and gives absolution in Christ's name. *174*

55. Does our sin only affect God?

No. When someone sins, he not only offends God; his sin

also has an effect, either direct or indirect, on other people. The priest who grants God's forgiveness also represents the whole Christian community, the church. Hence, the priest has the authority to reconcile a sinner to the body of Christ, the church. *174*

56. Is forgiveness the only benefit we can expect from confession?

The priest is often able to counsel and encourage the penitent, or even pray with the penitent for healing of some area of sin or brokenness in the person's life. *174*

57. What must we confess?

All mortal (serious) sins must be confessed, such as all serious sexual sins; conscious, serious rebellion against God; murder, and blasphemy. These and other mortal sins always must be confessed, while other sins we commit are called venial and are less serious in nature. But it is very helpful to confess our sins regularly—even if none of them are serious—so we can receive God's mercy, and his grace through the sacrament of reconciliation as an aid to avoiding sin.

58. What is meant by "mortal sin"?

Mortal sins are serious, deadly sins that break a person's friendship with God, or further deepen that rift or alienation between the person and God (1 Jn 5:16–17). In order for a sin to be mortal the person must be fully responsible for the act, deliberately and knowingly engaging in an act that seriously violates God's will and law, and hence deliberately turns the person away from God. Commiting a mortal sin entails both the person's awareness that the act is gravely wrong, and a substantially free decision to do it.

Once one commits mortal sin, he or she remains in the "state of mortal sin" until the person repents of this to God. The state of mortal sin is a state of estrangement or alienation from God. Rather than accepting the love and friendship that God has for each person, the person bound by mortal sin refuses God's love and friendship. *217*

59. What are the "seven deadly sins"?
Pride, greed, lust, anger, gluttony, envy, and sloth are the seven deadly sins. These sins are called "deadly" because they are at the root of so many other sins and because these sins quickly "deaden" our consciences. *217*

60. Must we confess less serious sins?
Less serious sins, often called "venial sins," injure our relationship with God but do not totally sever it. It is good, though not necessary, to confess all venial sins in the sacrament of reconciliation. *218*

61. Are those who confess their sins without real contrition, who just go through the motions, forgiven by God?
Contrition or sorrow for one's sins is necessary for absolution, but it is not necessary to feel great emotion. To feel sorrow for one's sins out of fear of hell is called attrition and, as such, it is sufficient for God's forgiveness. However, a scornful or impenitent attitude offends God and renders one liable for judgment (Is 29:13; Gal 6:7).

62. How should one approach the sacrament in order to receive the full effect of God's grace?
The penitent should be truly sorry for his or her sins because they offend God, and should have a willingness to make amends and do penance. The Catholic church recommends that the penitent make a thorough and honest "examination of conscience" before going to confession, reviewing all possible areas of sin. In fact, it is helpful to make such an "examination of conscience" regularly, even daily. The confession itself should be humble, thorough,

and honest. This attitude will enable the penitent to receive the full effect of God's forgiveness (Ps 51).

Anointing of the Sick

63. What is the anointing of the sick?

This sacrament carries on Jesus' own ministry of healing by prayer and anointing of the sick person for restoration of health. It also prepares a person on the verge of death to enter the Lord's presence when he or she dies. 174

64. How is the sacrament of the anointing of the sick found in Scripture?

Jesus healed the sick, and he commanded and empowered his disciples to do the same (Mk 6:13; Jas 5:14–15). The Bible explicitly teaches that the elders of the church should be called to pray over the sick and anoint them with oil for healing and forgiveness. 174–175

65. Isn't this sacrament also called the "Last Rites" or "Extreme Unction"?

In the past, this sacrament was usually administered immediately before death. It was the last rite the sick person received, hence the name "Last Rite" or "Extreme Unction" came to be associated with the anointing of the sick. Nowadays, the focus of the sacrament is on prayer for physical and spiritual strengthening or healing for all seriously ill persons, not only those at the point of death. 175

66. Do all the sick who receive this sacrament recover?

No. There is no guarantee that every sick person will be healed in a particular way. Every sacrament is effective, though the healing may not be visibly apparent to us. It may take the form of a healing of the patient's spiritual disposition or attitude of heart, preparing him or her to die. God is a healing God, and he often responds to the prayer of Christians and works through the sacrament of the anointing of the sick to restore to health those who are suffering. *175*

Sacraments of Vocation: Marriage and Holy Orders

67. What is meant by a "vocation"?
Vocation means to be "called." God gives each man and woman a calling, a particular state in life through which the person can become holy in service to God and others. *176*

68. Are any vocations also sacraments?
Two vocations are consecrated to God in a special way through the sacraments of the church: ordination to the ministerial priesthood and marriage. *176*

69. Why are marriage and holy orders considered to be indissoluble or permanent in the Catholic church?
When these sacraments are legitimately entered into and carried out, they are a sign of Christ's own love for the church and his life. Jesus himself taught that marriage is permanent (Mt 19:6) and the Old Testament says of priesthood, "You are a priest for ever / after the order of Melchizedek" (Ps 110:4). *176*

70. Why is marriage a sacrament?
Though marriage existed long before Christianity, marriage in Christ Jesus models the New Covenant between Jesus Christ and the church (Eph 5:22–33). The relationship of a married couple is a sacred covenant, a solemn promise involving the man, the woman, and God himself at the center of their union (Mt 19:3–9). *176–177*

71. Who is the minister of the sacrament of marriage?
The priest does not marry the couple, the man and woman marry each other. The priest or deacon is the church's witness to the covenant they make before God.

72. What are the signs of the sacrament?
The church requires the exchange of vows between man and woman made before the pastor or his delegate. There are two elements that constitute the one sign of matrimony: the mutual consent to wed and the conjugal act (sexual intercourse by the married couple).

73. What are the two benefits of marriage?
The Catholic church recognizes procreation (the bearing of children) and conjugal love (that is, faithful, mutual love and support within the marriage convenant) as the two greatest benefits of marriage. *177*

74. Should Catholic couples have children?
As part of their marriage covenant, Catholic couples vow to receive children lovingly from God. Children are the normal and precious fruit of Christian marriage, unless the couple is unable to conceive children. *177–178*

75. Are there special graces for the married couple in the sacrament?
Yes. Through the sacrament of marriage they receive the grace to love and remain faithful to the covenant and to carry out the duties of this state of life with the Spirit of Christ. They also receive grace to bring up any children they may be blessed with in the faith of the church and for the service of God. *177–178*

76. What is the sacrament of holy orders?
Based on the example of Jesus Christ, the church continues to call forth and set apart men to carry on the mission

of the apostles (Lk 22:29; Jn 20:21–23). This sacrament is conferred through the laying on of hands by a bishop, an anointing with blessed oil, and prayer. *180*

77. What is the mission of the priest or bishop?
The mission is threefold: 1) to proclaim, teach, and guard the word of God found in Scripture and authentic Catholic tradition, with the authority of Christ; 2) to carry on the priestly ministry of Jesus by presiding over the Eucharist or Lord's Supper, and as the normal minister of the other sacraments while acting in the person of Christ; 3) to shepherd and govern God's people according to the example of Jesus, the Good Shepherd, and according to his word and teaching. *181*

78. What is the difference between a priest's and a bishop's ordination?
Both have received the sacrament of holy orders. The ordination or consecration of a bishop is recognized by the Catholic church as the fullness of the sacrament of holy orders. Priests and deacons work with the bishop as shepherds of God's people. Their faculties are an extension of the bishop's authority in his diocese. Both priests and bishops are united in priestly dignity. *180*

79. What is a deacon?
The word deacon means servant. It was one of the first distinct leadership roles in the church (Acts 6:2–6). There are two types of deacons. The diaconate is the final preparatory stage before a man becomes a priest. The permanent diaconate has been recently restored as an active ordained leadership role in the church for married or single men. Deacons are ordained to a ministry of service, not to the priesthood. *98*

80. What role do deacons have in the church?

Deacons can minister the sacraments of baptism and matrimony and perform many other services for the church, including many liturgical functions such as reading the Gospel and preaching homilies at Mass. They may also serve the church in other significant ways. For example, they may be assigned important administrative responsibilities in caring for the life of a parish.

81. Are priests given special graces to sustain them in their vocation?

Yes. God provides all the graces needed to enable the priest to carry out his vocation faithfully and successfully. Priests also are aided in their vocation by the human support, prayers, and encouragement of other priests and lay persons. *181*

82. Why is celibacy required for ordination and priesthood?

Although celibacy is not a doctrinal requirement for priesthood, as married priests in Eastern Catholic churches testify, it is a discipline of the Roman Catholic church that has clear biblical precedent and has borne much good fruit over the centuries in the evident holiness and freedom for service of so many bishops and priests (Mt 19:12; 1 Cor 7:35). The Roman Catholic church follows the example and invitation of Jesus Christ, the great high priest, in upholding the discipline of celibacy for the ministerial priesthood. *182*

83. How are men chosen to serve as deacons, priests, or bishops?

God calls individual men to take up the call to ordained priesthood (2 Cor 10:18). Once a man has discerned this call through prayer and counsel, he submits this to the church for its discernment. If the church recognizes this as truly a call from God, he enters a period of training and preparation. *176, 180–182*

84. Do priests receive their authority to minister and govern from the people in the church?

No. The power and authority of the ministerial priesthood is given by the laying on of hands from God working through the pope and the bishops.

85. Why does the Catholic church ordain only men to the priesthood?

The Catholic church bases this practice primarily on the example of Jesus and nearly two thousand years of unbroken tradition, as well as on various other theological reasons. Although Jesus disregarded many of the social conventions of his day in the way he presented women with his message and called them to discipleship, he did not select a woman to be among the twelve apostles nor to be present at the Last Supper when he inaugurated the priesthood. The Catholic church has understood this for its entire history as an indication that it is not God's will that women be ordained to the priesthood. The sacramental or sign value of holy orders also dictates that the one who acts publicly in *persona Christi*, in the person of Christ, should resemble Christ. This is more clearly reflected by a man.

86. Does this mean that the Catholic church thinks less of women than of men?

Not at all. The Catholic church has consistently upheld the dignity of women and motherhood, praised and exalted consecrated virginity, and insisted upon the fundamental human and spiritual equality of women and men in Christ (Gal 3:28). The Catholic church has emphasized the complementarity of the gifts and roles of women and men in marriage and in the life of the church and society. *177, 178*

SIX

Prayer, Devotions, and the Holy Spirit

1. Do we need to pray?
Yes! No relationship can continue or grow without commu-nication. Prayer is a two-way communication with God: we speak to him and God speaks to us. Christians need to set aside a time every day to focus on God, to speak to him, and to listen to him. *183*

2. How should we pray?
Christians are to approach God simply, directly, humbly, and unpretentiously as seen in the Lord's Prayer (Lk 11:2). *183–184*

3. When and how often should Christians pray?
Scripture teaches the need to pray continually (Lk 18:1f; 1 Thes 5:17; Eph 6:18). There are many methods to achieve this, but the goal always remains the same: to be aware of God's presence and to be constantly turning our thoughts and attention to him and to the accomplishment of his will. *184*

4. Is it important to devote a particular time each day to pray?
Yes. We need to focus our attention solely on God with a

minimum of distractions in order to grow in knowledge and love of God and in our ability to listen and understand his word. *184*

5. What elements should be in a daily prayer time?
a) Adoration: worship and praise of God. b) Thanksgiving: thanking God for his past and present blessings. c) Repentance: examining our conscience in order to recognize and turn from sin in order to receive God's forgiveness. d) Petition: asking God for our needs and those of the broader world and church. e) Listening: understanding what God requires of us. *185*

6. How does God speak to us?
God doesn't usually speak in an audible way, but rather through the thoughts and gentle urgings that the Holy Spirit stirs up in our minds and hearts. Important ways God speaks to us are: through his Word in the Scripture, through the writings of saints or of holy men and women, and through the members of his body on earth, the church (2 Tm 3:15–17). *185–186*

7. Is prayer with others important?
Personal prayer is the foundation of meaningful communal prayer, while communal prayer can enrich personal prayer. In communal prayer, we come together as God's people to fulfill our most exalted task—to worship and praise our Creator. All of our individual works, intentions, and needs are gathered together and brought to God when we join to worship as a united body. *188–189*

8. What kinds of communal prayer are there?
The official public prayer of the Catholic church is known as liturgical prayer. Liturgy is led by an ordained minister of the church. There are also informal gatherings of Christians who join in various forms of shared prayer. These

include rosaries and novenas prayed together, prayer breakfasts, prayer meetings, fellowship groups, and others. These non-liturgical activities can be led by someone other than an ordained Catholic minister. *189*

9. Can informal gatherings be substituted for attending Mass?
No. They are supplemental to the official, liturgical worship of the Catholic church. *189*

10. What is liturgical prayer?
Liturgy is the official communal prayer of the whole church joined to Christ its head, in perpetual prayer before the Father. The word *liturgy* literally means the "work" or "service" of the people. To worship together is the primary work or service of God's people. *190*

11. What is the highest form of liturgical prayer?
The Eucharist or Mass is the highest form of liturgical prayer. The unity of the church, including our unity with God and with one another, finds its fullest expression in the celebration of the death and resurrection of Christ in the Eucharist, because it makes present the one perfect, acceptable offering and sacrifice to the Father through his own Son Jesus Christ in the power of the Holy Spirit. *191*

12. Are there other forms of liturgical prayer?
Yes. There are three main forms: a) the Liturgy of the Hours is the official daily prayer of the church; b) Benediction focuses on worshiping the Lord present in the Blessed Sacrament, the reserved eucharistic Host; c) the communal celebration of the various sacraments is also liturgical prayer. *191*

13. What should be our attitude as we approach the liturgy?
Common worship requires faith and our active participation. It is not enough simply to be present physically and to go through the motions. *191*

14. What are common elements of liturgical celebrations?
Sacred Scripture and various forms of prayer or rites are always incorporated in every form of liturgy. Music, art, and other supportive elements are often included as well. *191*

15. Isn't liturgical prayer too formal because most of its prayers are determined?
One of the aspects of the beauty of the liturgy is its universality, that it is the common prayer of Catholics throughout the world. Yet Catholic liturgy can never be totally uniform or rigid, because within the liturgy there is room for legitimate variation. For example, there are now four different Eucharistic prayers, and special canons for children and reconciliation. Various responses can be said or chanted. There are many different "votive" Masses for special occasions as well as optional prayers to celebrate the feasts of particular saints. The musical options alone permit a great deal of variation. The faith of the living community and the presence of the Holy Spirit also bring new life to liturgical prayers. *192*

16. Isn't spontaneous worship more pleasing to God because "the written code kills but the Spirit gives life" (2 Cor 3:6)?
If liturgical prayer is ever deadening, it is not because it is dead, but because we have not fully come alive to God or to what we are doing when we worship together as his people. Even spontaneous prayer repeated again and again often becomes very unspontaneous and rigid. *192*

17. Why is the Mass the center of Catholic liturgical prayer?
Because the Mass recalls and represents (presents once again in sacramental form) the greatest event of history and of Christian faith: the paschal mystery—the passion, death, resurrection and ascension of our Lord and Savior Jesus Christ. *193*

18. Has the Mass always been celebrated as it is today?
Though there has been development over the years, the primitive form of the Mass and its prayers are strikingly close to the basic format of the Mass today. *193–194*

19. What is the structure of the Mass?
There are two basic parts: the Liturgy of the Word, and the Liturgy of the Eucharist. *194–195*

20. What is the Liturgy of the Word?
The introductory rites, including a time of repentance, the Gloria, two or three readings from Scripture, and the homily are all part of the Liturgy of the Word. *195*

21. What is the purpose of the homily?
The homily or sermon proclaims the ways God has worked in the history of salvation, especially through the mystery of Christ. The content of the homily is to be drawn from biblical and liturgical sources. The entire Liturgy of the Word prepares us to fittingly worship God and receive the body and blood of Christ in the Eucharist. *195*

22. How should I expect God's word to apply to my life?
Because Scripture is the Word of God, it is never irrelevant or outmoded in anything that pertains to salvation, faith in God, and morality (Jn 10:35). It is a living Word, that is, capable of speaking to our situation and of revealing new depths and insights every time we encounter it. We can

expect to come to understand who God is and know ourselves better. We also see how to live our lives more in conformity with the gospel.

23. What is the Liturgy of the Eucharist?
The Liturgy of the Eucharist begins, on Sundays or holy days, with the profession of the faith, the prayers of the faithful, includes the offertory, centers on the great Eucharistic Prayer during which the consecration of the bread and wine take place, is followed by the recitation of the Lord's Prayer, the kiss of peace, and communion. A period of prayer and reflection follows communion. Mass ends with concluding prayers and the dismissal. *195–197*

24. How can we grow closer to God?
Prayer, the sacraments, and the study of God's Word in the Bible and in authentic Christian tradition are the basic ways that God has given humanity to grow in union with him. However, there are many other helps that assist us in living a fuller, richer Christian life. *197*

25. What is the liturgical year?
The liturgical year designates periods of time to reflect upon the major events of Jesus Christ's life. It is an important way that Catholics continually are enabled to recall and live out the mysteries of our salvation in Jesus Christ. *198–200*

26. What are the major liturgical seasons?
Advent, Christmas, Lent, and Easter. Ordinary time focuses on the events and teaching of Jesus' public ministry and culminates in the teaching on the end of time and on his second coming. *198–199*

27. What is the Liturgy of the Hours?
The Liturgy of the Hours or Divine Office is the official daily liturgical prayer of the whole Catholic church. It is

comprised mainly of the recitation of psalms, readings from the Bible, and some selections from distinguished church fathers and conciliar (documents of church councils) statements of the past. *200–201*

28. Why do Catholics venerate the saints?
An important aspect of both the Jewish and Christian tradition has been to honor and praise the godly men and women who have gone before us (Sir 44). One reason for this is to receive encouragement from their example and to imitate their virtues (Heb 11–12:4). Another reason is that we may receive help from their prayers as they remember our particular needs before the throne of God. *201*

29. What is a saint?
Those whom the Catholic church believe were united to the Lord in heaven immediately upon death are declared to be saints. The witness of their lives, works, and writings serve as exemplary models of Christian life and virtue.

30. Doesn't St. Paul refer to all Christians as "saints" or "holy ones"?
Yes. As baptized Christians, we all share in the holiness of the church and in the communion of the saints. We are all called to personal holiness and in this sense, we can all be called saints. But the Catholic church gives the title *saint* to a man or woman who is recognized to have been particularly close to God because of a life of faith and obedience, and about whom there is a certainty of salvation. *201*

31. How does the Catholic church decide who is a saint?
The process by which the Catholic church formally recognizes a deceased person as a saint is called "canonization." The person's life, works, and writings are examined and testimony gathered from those who knew him or her to determine if extraordinary sanctity was evident.

32. Doesn't attention given to the saints or requesting their prayers detract from the worship due to God alone?
No. The Catholic church cautions believers that their devotion to Mary or the saints should in no way contradict or detract from the adoration given to God alone. Younger children in a family look up to their older brothers and sisters and seek their help and advice. Of course this does not diminish their love or respect for their father. Proper devotion to Mary or the saints is to be encouraged because we are members of the family of God. We must always approach God with our needs through Jesus Christ, the "one mediator between God and men" (1 Tm 2:5), in the power of the Holy Spirit. 202

33. What are devotions?
A devotion is a Christian's personal dedication to a saint or to an aspect of the life of Christ or Mary which is a special inspiration to the person, and to whom the individual may feel an affinity. This attitude of devotion may give rise to particular practices that emphasize the role of the saint or mystery in the individual's life. Prayers directed to Jesus under such titles as the "Sacred Heart," or to Mary as the "Immaculate Conception" or "Queen of Peace," or other titles are examples of devotions. Specific types of prayers such as the rosary, consecration to Mary or the Sacred Heart, novenas, or chaplets are also called devotions. 203

34. Why can it be helpful to have a devotion to a particular saint or mystery of the faith?
Praying and reflecting on heavenly realities may inspire a person and draw him or her closer to God. Just as in a family there are special bonds between certain members, in God's family there often develop special bonds of spiritual unity and friendship among members of the church. Sometimes apostolates (groups, like religious, with a special vocation in the church) include the name of a particu-

lar saint or mystery in their title in order to place their work under that saint's special intercession or to reflect the focus of their work. *202*

35. What is the rosary?
The rosary is a series of prayers that accompany prayerful reflection on the fifteen mysteries of the life of Christ and his mother. It is the most popular non-liturgical devotion among many Catholics. *203*

36. What are sacramentals?
As their name implies, sacramentals usually are related to one of the seven sacraments. Like the sacraments, sacramentals make use of material objects to remind us of God and to put us into contact with him through our senses. They differ from sacraments in that their effectiveness in drawing us closer to God depends more on our personal faith and devotion. *204*

37. What is fasting?
Fasting is a form of self-denial. Christians deny themselves food, drink, sleep or comfort, not because the body is evil or demands punishment, but a) as a form of prayer of petition to God; b) to remind us of God's goodness and of our utter dependence on him; and c) to detach ourselves temporarily from some good things of the world in order to focus more fully on God and to hear him speak to us more clearly (Mk 2:18–20; Acts 13:2; 14:23; 2 Cor 11:27). The self-mastery that comes from such penitential practices frees one to follow God more easily. *205*

38. What is abstinence?
To refrain from eating meat for a designated length of time. It is particular type of self-denial.

39. When should Catholics fast?

The *Didache*, an early Christian writing, records that Christians fasted on Wednesdays and Fridays. Today many Catholics fast on Fridays. The Catholic church teaches that fast and abstinence are to be practiced, especially during the penitential season of Lent. *205*

40. What are the guidelines for fasting and abstinence?

Catholics are encouraged to take more responsiblity in this area and to undertake penances voluntarily. Lenten guidelines set Ash Wednesday and Good Friday as days of fast and abstinence and all Fridays within Lent as days of abstinence. However the new Code of Canon Law still encourages Catholics to fast voluntarily on every Friday.

41. What is penance?

Penance is an act of self-denial or mortification in not only food but in other areas as well. It includes prayer and charity, especially giving alms, i.e., money to those in need. *206*

42. What are indulgences?

The Catholic church declares that special graces, called "indulgences," may come to a baptized person who offers certain prayers or who performs certain penitential works with the intention of receiving these special graces. True faith and love of God must be a motivating factor in seeking an indulgence. These indulgences are a special share in the "infinite merits of Christ," for the removal of the temporal punishment due to sin. *206*

43. What is "temporal punishment due to sin"?

The sinner normally experiences the consequences of his or her sin as a punishment that comes upon the person either in this life or after death in purgatory. Sin, as a rejection of God, necessarily brings with it painful consequences or side-effects. *206*

44. Isn't the merit of Christ's death enough to forgive us our sins?
Yes, it is. However, the forgiveness of sins does not necessarily take away its consequences in our lives spiritually, relationally or physically. For example, if a basement is flooded, a new drain will take away the water but not the damage that the water has done. Even forgiven sins leave "watermarks," or effects and bad habits in our lives that must be overcome by good ones. *206–207*

45. Can one gain indulgences only for oneself?
No. Christians not only can seek these indulgences for themselves but also for others in the body of Christ, even for the deceased who may still be suffering the consequences of their own sin in purgatory. *207*

46. What is the source and foundation of all Christian prayer?
The Catholic church teaches that it is impossible to pray or have a life of true devotion without the Holy Spirit (Jn 4:23, 24). *207*

47. How are we to relate to the Holy Spirit?
Christians are to relate to the Holy Spirit as a person—as the person of God who guides us (Acts 16:6–8); speaks to us (Acts 10:19; 13:2; 21:11; 28:25); consoles us (Acts 9:31); sends us forth (Acts 13:4); warns us (Acts 20:23); prompts (Acts 21:4); and teaches us the truth (Jn 16:13). *212*

48. Are there gifts of the Holy Spirit?
Yes. There are three categories of gifts of the Holy Spirit: the Isaian, the Pauline, and the fruits of the Holy Spirit. *210–212*

49. What are the Isaian gifts?
The Isaian gifts are wisdom, understanding, counsel, knowledge, fortitude, piety, and fear of the Lord (Is 11:2–3). These gifts are received at confirmation and are intended for the personal growth and guidance of the individual believer. *210*

50. What are the Pauline gifts?
Some of the Pauline gifts are the word of wisdom, the word of knowledge, faith, healing, miracles, prophecy, discernment of spirits, tongues, interpretation of tongues, and others (1 Cor 12:4–11). Paul's list is not intended to be exhaustive. These are also called the *charisms* or charismatic gifts. They are intended for the building up of the body of Christ. *211*

51. What are the fruits of the Spirit?
The fruits of the Spirit are: love, joy, peace, patience, kindness, goodness, faithfulness, gentleness, self-control (Gal 5:22, 23). They are the characteristics of the mature Christian, modeling Christ-like character for us. *212*

52. Why does the Holy Spirit give us these gifts?
God, through his Holy Spirit, lavishes these gifts on his children out of an abundance of love, with the goal of enabling each person and the whole church to become mature in Christ.

53. What is the value of the gifts and graces of the Holy Spirit?
The value of these workings of the Spirit are always determined by the way they are used and their end or purpose. They must be used in love (1 Cor 13), and their highest purpose is the common good of the church (Eph 4:11–12). They are never to be considered as personal property or cause for boasting as they are free gifts of God. *212*

54. What is the role of the Holy Spirit in the church?

The Holy Spirit is given by God to be the font of the church's life, love, and power. The role of the Holy Spirit in the church is to create and safeguard the unity of Christians and the church (1 Cor 12:12–27); to lead the church to the fullness of truth (Jn 16:13); and to remain in the church as God's continuing presence, both in individual members and in the body of Christ as a whole. *212, 95*

55. What is the "baptism of the Holy Spirit"?

Although this expression has a specific biblical meaning, it commonly refers to a new release of the Holy Spirit that many Christians experience in their lives. Some of the signs of being baptized in the Spirit are: a new awareness of God and a deeper relationship with him; a new ability to understand Scripture; new fervor and meaning to personal prayer and participation in the sacraments; and a more fervent love of God. In addition, some Christians experience certain charismatic gifts of the Spirit released in their lives for the first time or in a new way. *208–210*

56. How is the extra-sacramental working of the Holy Spirit to be understood theologically by Catholics?

Baptism in the Holy Spirit is not an eighth sacrament. The primary meaning of the baptism of the Holy Spirit is to bring the believer into a living knowledge and faith in God as Father, Son, and Holy Spirit. The believer no longer just knows about God, he or she knows God in a new way. Baptism by water, in the name of the Trinity, introduces us into a life of faith in God. Confirmation is understood as the empowering of the believer to witness to God and serve him faithfully. Baptism in the Holy Spirit does not replace either of these two sacraments. Rather, it can be understood as a result of these graces in the believer, or as a fuller release or experience of graces already received. *209*

SEVEN

Living as a Catholic Christian

1. What is the goal of life for Catholic Christians?
We are most fully Catholic and Christian when we strive to become like Jesus Christ in our thoughts, words, and deeds. *216*

2. Does God expect Christians primarily to avoid sin and doing evil?
Certainly this is true, but the Christian call is even more positive and challenging: to become like Christ, to grow in the virtues that characterize his life by the power of the Holy Spirit. *216*

3. Why do we find it so difficult to become like Christ?
Because of sin. Personal sin not only injures and disfigures us, but it offends God. If we live according to our sinful nature, we cannot be like Jesus Christ. *217*

4. Is it possible to overcome personal sin and choose to follow Christ?
Yes. God has made it possible for us through the grace and reconciliation won for us by Jesus Christ's death on the cross. *218–219*

5. How do we know we are indeed following God?
Modern theology speaks about this choice as a person's "fundamental option." This theory stresses that the basic orientation of a person's life is either toward God, through obedience to God in response to his grace, or away from God, due to serious sin. According to this moral theory, it is possible for a person oriented toward God to offend God in small ways and yet remain in God's friendship. *219*

6. Then venial sins do not matter?
The person's fundamental option may not change, despite some failures and shortcomings. However, many small sins do weaken our relationship with God and may lead us to fall into more serious sin that separates us from God's friendship; this changes our fundamental option. Christians cannot take venial sin lightly. Besides, all sin offends God and rebels against his loving plan for us. *219*

7. How does one change his fundamental option toward God instead of away from him?
Sometimes people who have rejected God can do genuinely good things. This is a sign that God may be at work in their lives to lead them to conversion. Conversion involves a choice to accept God's offer of forgiveness through repentance and seeks to turn back to God in the small acts of daily life. *219*

8. What is repentance?
Repentance is to renounce all evil and to turn toward God, seeking his forgiveness and changing one's way of life to conform to his will. The word is taken from the Greek *metanoia*, which literally means to "change your mind" about the way you are living and accept God's judgment and will. *222–223*

9. What if God does not forgive our sins?
God always forgives the sins of those who sincerely repent. *223*

10. How does conversion differ from repentance?
Conversion is part of repentance. As we turn away from sin, we must turn toward God in Jesus Christ by believing in him and submitting our lives to him and to his plan for us. *223*

11. How does conversion come about?
Some people have a sudden conversion experience in which they radically turned away from sin and turned to God in a single grace-filled moment. Conversion may be more gradual and take place in progressive stages. Actually, Christians are always in the need of deeper, ongoing conversion (Lk 9:23–24). *223–224*

12. What are the three enemies of God that we struggle against as we seek to become like Christ?
Classical Catholic teaching recognizes that the three main obstacles to living as a Christian are the world, the flesh, and the devil. *219*

13. What is meant by the "world"?
The world in this sense is not the created order nor the world which God came to save. Rather it is a biblical term for that world or world system of human ideas and values that are opposed to God and his rule (Jn 17:9; 1 Jn 2:15). *220*

14. Is the world, in this sense, always abstract ideas and philosophies?
No. It can refer to excessive attraction or attachment to things or ideas in the world, even though these things may be good in themselves. Especially in Western society,

the most powerful and seductive example of the world is materialism, the ceaseless pursuit of material things and the quenchless desire for still more. 220

15. What is the "flesh"?
This is not our physical flesh or bodies, which are good because they are created by God, but flesh in the Pauline sense of the sensual attractions of our fallen human nature (Gal 5:19–21, 24). It is a distortion of basic human drives and appetites that are essentially good, such as the desire for food, rest, or sexual fulfillment. Thus, we indulge these appetites in ways apart from God's plan, so that we become enslaved to them rather than controlling them as their masters. *220*

16. How can the devil oppose us, since Christ robbed Satan of victory by his death on the cross?
Although Satan was defeated and all his power broken by Jesus' death and resurrection, in the mystery of God's plan, God still permits Satan and other evil spiritual powers to tempt humanity until Christ's glorious second coming (Rv 20).

Until Christ returns again at the end of time, the world is still bound to some degree by the power and dominion of Satan (1 Jn 5:19). However, Satan's power is broken when people turn to God and receive his life and power through Jesus Christ. Through our free decisions to follow God's plan and ways, the dominion of Satan on the earth is broken, and the kingdom of God advances. This is a primary result of the mission and ministry of Jesus and his church. *220–221*

17. How can Christians withstand the wiles of the devil?
By prayer, watchfulness, and spiritual warfare (1 Pt 5:8–9; Jas 4:7–8; Jn 17:15; Eph 6:10–13). The church has consistently recommended the frequent reception of the sacra-

ments of reconciliation and the Eucharist and praying that God forms his character in us as powerful means of overcoming the evil one. We must, however, cooperate with the grace he offers us through these channels. *221, 224*

18. Should we be afraid of the devil?
No. We have no reason to fear him or evil spirits. Jesus Christ has overcome all evil, and we need only draw near to Christ in prayer and faith and daily put on the "whole armor of God" (Eph 6:14–18) to find protection from Satan and the spiritual powers of evil. We can also ask the intercession of Mary, St. Michael the Archangel, and all the saints and angels. *221–222*

19. What is the Catholic teaching on the occult or astrology?
The Catholic teaching on the occult or any form of spiritism (including astrology) is clear: we should avoid it. We should have nothing to do with even seemingly harmless or entertaining forms of the occult such as ouija boards, seances, automatic writing, and any kind of fortune telling. *222*

20. How can we cooperate with God?
We can seek to assume the character and virtues of Christ through discipline and by our decisions to act or think in certain ways, while always realizing that, ultimately, only God can develop our character and infuse virtues. *224*

21. What are the "theological" virtues?
Faith, hope, and charity or love are called *theological* because they are the main Christian virtues that direct us to God. The apostle Paul teaches they will not pass away but will be fully realized in love, which is the most excellent of the three (1 Cor 13:13). *224–225*

22. What is charity?

Love is the very essence of God's nature (1 Jn 4:8). All the other virtues spring from love and end in love because love gives them their meaning. *225*

23. Describe faith.

Faith is the only proper orientation toward God through which we are justified, that is, considered righteous in God's sight (Rom 4:24–25), and sanctified, that is, made holy, or like God. *225*

24. What is hope?

Hope is the firm confidence God gives to a person that he or she will persevere in faith and love and so attain eternal life and happiness with God. Hope is also communal because it is the hope of the whole Christian people that Christ's desire is to save us, bringing all who are faithful to God and his grace to the glory of heaven. *225*

25. Is hope only good when directed toward eternal life?

No. We also hope in God's mercy and blessings for his people in this life on earth, although this is not the ultimate goal of hope (1 Cor 15:19). *225*

26. What are "cardinal" virtues?

Cardinal or moral virtues are prudence, justice, fortitude, and temperance. They reflect aspects of the central virtues of faith, hope, and love. These virtues are primarily meant to help us in our daily life, while the theological virtues are meant to orient us primarily toward God. Prudence enables one to choose correctly how to best carry out the will of God. Justice inclines us to give to others at all times what is due to them by right. Fortitude or courage enables the Christian to do what is right and required in the Christian life, whatever the cost or consequences. Temperance or self-control is a virtue which enables us to control our bodily desires and appetites, especially our sexual powers and appetite for food and drink. *226*

27. Are there other virtues besides these?
Yes. We recognize under different names other virtues such as the beatitudes (Mt 5:2–12), and the "fruit of the Spirit" (Gal 5:22–23). *226*

28. How do all of these virtues develop in our lives?
These virtues develop through practice in response to God's grace until they become mature habits, intrinsic parts of the Christian character. If we lack any of these virtues, we should pray for them and seek to practice them in our daily lives. *226*

29. What are "works of mercy"?
They are living expressions of virtue. Catholic theology notes that some of these works serve the physical and practical needs of others (the "corporal works of mercy") and some meet the spiritual needs of others (the "spiritual works of mercy"). Corporal works of mercy are: to feed the hungry, to give drink to the thirsty, to clothe the naked, to shelter the homeless, to visit the imprisoned, to care for the sick, and to bury the dead (Mt 25:31–36). The spiritual works of mercy are: to admonish the sinner, to instuct the ignorant, to advise the perplexed, to comfort the sorrow-ful, to bear wrongs patiently, to forgive all injuries, and to pray for the living and the dead. *227*

30. What is "sanctifying grace"?
Sanctifying grace is the living presence of Christ and the Holy Spirit within us. This saving grace leads to our sancti-fication throughout life, as we respond to it in faith. Through baptism and the other sacraments, we come to share the very life of God, which Catholics call "sanctify-ing grace." *227*

31. What is "prevenient grace"?
This is God's grace which comes before every good thought or action, and even every inclination to the good. *227*

32. What is "actual grace"?
It is the power God offers us each day to avoid sin and to do his will in particular circumstances. *227*

33. What is the "grace of final perseverance"?
It is the ability to continue to follow Jesus Christ to the end of our lives so we will be able to share eternal life with him in heaven. Catholics believe that it is possible for a person to fall away from God and to forfeit the gift of salvation, so the grace of final perseverance is necessary to insure that a person will be saved. *227*

34. Do we have to accept God's grace?
God's grace is never forced upon anyone. It must be sought after and freely accepted. *227*

35. Are any of our virtues or good works due to our human will or effort, or are they entirely the work of God?
No Christian can boast of any good work as being his own (Eph 2:8–10; 1 Cor 1:31; 2 Cor 10:17). God, through his grace, is the primary source and author of every virtue and good work. On the other hand, the active cooperation of the human will with God's grace is essential. *227–228*

36. Are we responsible for our actions since God's grace is essential?
Yes. The Catholic church has always maintained the reality of free will that makes possible real human responsiblity for our choices and actions. Every good human act is both a result of God's action and his grace and the free response of the human will to God's grace in performing the act. *228*

37. When we sin, does that mean God failed to give us enough grace?

No. God always offers us sufficient grace to resist temptation and choose the right response to every situation. However, this may be very difficult when the will is weakened or blinded by sin, especially habitual patterns of sin.

38. What is meant by "conscience"?

Conscience is the core of a person's being, the faculty by which he makes practical judgments about whether particular acts are morally right or wrong. *228*

39. Are Catholics obliged to follow the dictates of their consciences?

Yes, a person is bound to follow his own conscience, whether correct or incorrect, because the conscience is the only internal faculty by which a person can judge what is right and wrong. However, this indicates that each person is morally obligated both to inform the conscience of what is truly right and wrong, and to search the conscience to determine what is good and evil in cases where a decision or judgment must be made.

God assists us in both of these tasks through the light of the Holy Spirit. In his encyclical letter on the Holy Spirit, Pope John Paul II calls the Holy Spirit the "light of consciences," who enables the conscience to recognize the truth and to make right judgments. *229*

40. What if one makes the wrong decision, is he responsible?

If individuals do their best to form their conscience according to God's will, they can err but are not guilty of negligence or sin. If a person is ignorant or in error in a moral decision because of negligence in seeking the truth, God holds the person responsible for this. *229*

41. How is a person's conscience formed correctly?
First, the Catholic church believes there are reliable, objective sources through which God reveals his will. These include divine revelation, natural law, official church teaching, and human law. The practice of frequent prayer and of Christian virtue and works of mercy previously discussed also help form the conscience according to God's will, as does the continual effort to follow the leadings of the Holy Spirit in everyday life. *230*

42. What other ways can Catholics properly form their conscience?
They can foster proper dispositions and attitudes of the mind and heart. For example, one must desire to know the truth and be willing to accept it, whether it is immediately agreeable or not. Catholics must seek to have a positive attitude toward legitimate authority and be willing to be taught by the church. *230*

43. What three aspects should a person consider before making a decision?
1) The object: Does the act itself conform to the moral law? Is the act good in itself according to God's revelation through objective sources?
2) Circumstances: Are there any relevant circumstances that may affect the degree of rightness or wrongness of the act?
3) The end or purpose: Is the intention behind performing the act a genuinely good one? Does the act have a good end or purpose? *All three* of these aspects must be positive for the act or decision to be assuredly a good one. *230–231*

44. Can the moral value of an act be determined almost entirely by the situation or circumstances?
No. This is often called "situation ethics," and Catholic teaching rejects this view. Even though circumstances may affect the decision or may lessen or increase the person's culpability (blameworthiness) for a wrong act, circumstances cannot make an act right which is wrong or evil in itself (the object) or which is done with an evil or selfish intention (the end or purpose). *231*

45. Can you give an example of that?
Suppose a married couple consider using artificial contraceptives because they have a low income and a large family. However, the Catholic church teaches that this means of birth regulation is wrong or objectionable in itself. Therefore, it cannot be morally justified to use artificial birth control even if one's intentions are good. The church has approved natural methods of birth regulation when rightly used, usually called Natural Family Planning. *231–232*

46. What if one doesn't agree with the teaching of the Catholic church?
Vatican II makes it clear that Catholics should approach the teachings of the pope, bishops, and other authorized teachers with an attitude of assent (submissiveness) and willingness to be taught by them. It is true that there are different degrees of authority of a church teaching. Those moral and religious teachings that have been formally defined by dogmatic definitions of popes or ecumenical councils of bishops are to be accepted by Catholics as part of our Christian faith as "articles of faith." Other teachings which have been consistently believed by Christians from the time of the early church until recent times must be accepted as part of the faith of the church as well. Many moral teachings of the Catholic church fall into this latter category, such as the condemnation of abortion, homosex-

ual acts, and masturbation. Even teachings of the bishops in union with the pope, or of the pope himself, that do not formally define doctrine should be readily accepted and adhered to, according to Vatican II (*Lumen Gentium* no. 25). 232

47. Can Catholics question or struggle with a formally defined church teaching and still be loyal to the church?
Yes, as long as they are seeking to fully understand why the church teaches as it does in order to follow that teaching wholeheartedly and with a clear conscience. The end result should be to recognize and personally embrace the truth of a teaching that is presented by the Catholic church as a dogmatic definition or a matter of faith. 232

48. Do Catholics have to accept all church teachings equally?
Our basic presupposition and attitude should be that what the pope and the bishops united with him teach is true, even matters that they do not formally define as Catholic doctrine, but which are part of their "Ordinary Magisterium" (usual or everyday teaching office). Even this "Ordinary Magisterium" would include some teachings that Catholics should accept as articles of faith because of their frequent repetition or general acceptance throughout the Catholic church's history. For example, the doctrine of the assumption of Mary into heaven had been widely acepted for centuries by Catholics as a truth of our faith, even before Pope Pius XII formally defined this doctrine in 1950.

Much of what is presented in the "Ordinary Magisterium" of the bishops or popes is considered "religious teaching"—teaching which is neither dogmatically defined nor universally believed, but teaching that should be heeded and accepted with an obedient attitude. Examples of such religious teachings would be the principle that an employer should pay his workers a just wage, or diocesan guidelines for fast and abstinence during Lent.

It is true that each person must ultimately follow his or her own conscience, but Catholics have a responsibility to form their consciences according to the church's teachings. In the instances in which a doctrine is defined infallibly by the pope or by an ecumenical council of bishops, or teachings have been frequently repeated and confirmed throughout the history of the church, these teachings *must* be given loyal and obedient assent by all the faithful. 233

49. Are God's laws arbitrary, subjective concepts?
Not at all. It only makes sense that the God who created the human race would also determine and then reveal the ways by which we would find true happiness and fulfillment. God himself clearly determined the realities of good and evil, right and wrong, as part of his work of creation. 235

50. What is "natural law"?
Natural law does not mean laws of nature, such as gravity, but the ways God created man to act and relate. These laws may be discovered or deduced from observing human nature itself. They are universal principles that apply to people of all times, places, cultures, and situations. Even sin cannot obscure our recognition of the truths of natural law. St. Thomas Aquinas, the great theologian who wrote the *Summa Theologica*, defined natural law as our participation in the eternal laws of God, inscribed in the basic constitution (order) of his creation, which urges us to do good and avoid evil. 235–237

51. What is an example of natural law?
Man and woman were created by God as two different sexes in order to procreate or reproduce. This points to the natural purpose and meaning of sexuality and indicates

that homosexuality and masturbation are distortions of the natural law in this area. 236

52. What is "divine law"?

This is God's plan for living given through revelation and grace, as through the inspired authors of the Bible. For example, the Ten Commandments or Decalogue (Ex 20:2–17; Dt 5:6–22) are essential commands revealed by God that are binding on all people at all times. 237

53. What is the greatest commandment?

The greatest commandment is to love God with all our heart, soul, and mind. The second is like it: to love our neighbor as ourselves (Mt 22:37–39; cf. Dt 6:4–5; Lv 19:18). Jesus summarized God's law and plan for our lives in these two points. 238

54. What is the minimum standard of conduct we must obey?

Jesus taught that we are not called by God to meet a minimum standard, but to the perfection of holiness and discipleship (Mt 5:48).

55. How are the biblical standards for life to be interpreted and applied properly to new circumstances?

Catholics believe that God provides such interpretation and application of Christian truth through the official teaching office (Magisterium) of the Catholic church. This teaching office both passes on and interprets the divine law as it comes to us through sacred Scripture and tradition, as well as providing guidance based on these sources for new issues that have not been addressed before.

Because of recent medical and technological advances the Catholic church has had to apply the principles of divine law to many new moral issues such as *in vitro* fertilization, artificial insemination, active and passive euthanasia, and so on. Magisterial documents such as the *Instruction on Respect for Human Life In Its Origin and the Dignity of Procreation: Replies to Certain Questions of the Day* (1987) and the *Declaration On Euthanasia* (1980) are excellent applications of biblical standards applied to modern circumstances. *240*

56. What role do parents and teachers play in passing on the faith?

Without teachers and parents actively understanding and explaining the Christian way of life and the faith of the church, few would actually hear what the Bible and the Magisterium has to say. The role of parents and teachers in passing on the Christian way of life is essential and irreplaceable. *241*

57. Is there a comphrehensive list of Catholic teachings on moral issues and what church teachings Catholics are bound to believe?

Although there is no definitive list of official pronouncements on moral teaching, many of them are summarized in documents such as *To Live in Christ Jesus* (1976) or *Basic Teachings for Catholic Religious Education* (1973), published in the United States by the National Conference of Catholic Bishops. A universal catechism which will provide clear guidelines for Catholic teaching is now being prepared. *241*

58. What role does human law have in our moral guidance?

Both civil and church law make up the final source of guidance for Christians. Human law, especially church law, can actually be an aid to observing the law of God. Because of fallen man's inclination to sin, human law can curb our tendency to sin and help us to follow God's will. *242*

59. What role does fellowship with other Christians have in living according to the will of God?

We cannot live a righteous moral life on our own. Besides the teaching and guidance of the church, we also need support and encouragement, and sometimes correction and admonition, from other Christians to spur us on to live according to God's will each day.

EIGHT

Catholics in the World

1. How does Vatican II describe the condition of the modern world?
The Second Vatican Council saw the world today in a position of dangerous paradox, with the future of the human race hanging in the balance depending upon the choices we make. *247–248*

2. What is the heart of the problem with the world today?
The basic problem of human life in the world today and always is the rejection of God, whether through knowing denial of God, through ignorance, or through the rebellion against him that Christians call sin. *249–250*

3. What is God's solution to the problems of the world?
The world's problems cannot be solved by human efforts alone. Sin has only one remedy, the redemptive love and mercy of God that comes to us through our Savior Jesus Christ. In Christ, each person has been given the opportunity to be transformed from within and reborn in the image of God, our Creator. *250–251*

4. What is one of the central goals of the Catholic church's efforts in relation to the world?
The Catholic church seeks to promote and safeguard the

dignity of each human person. The church is convinced that the solution to the problems of human society depends upon a correct understanding and appreciation of the unsurpassable worth of each human life. *253–254*

5. How valuable is the human person in the eyes of the Catholic church?

The Catholic church has always taught and defended the inestimable value of every human life, believing that each human person is more valuable in God's eyes than all other created things combined. *254*

6. Why do humans have so great a value?

Each human is given an inherent dignity and worth by God far beyond any other created thing because each human has an immortal soul, an intellect, a moral conscience, and the gift of free will. *254–255*

7. What rights and obligations necessarily follow from the dignity of the human person?

The Catholic church recognizes the following rights as applying to all people, at all times, in every place without exception: the basic necessities of human life, such as food, clothing, and shelter; the right to choose a state in life freely and to found a family; the rights to education, to gainful employment, to a good reputation, to respect, to appropriate information, to protection of privacy, and to rightful religious freedom. *255*

8. What are the violations of human dignity that the church strongly opposes?

The Catholic church opposes whatever is opposed to life itself, such as any type of murder, genocide, abortion, euthanasia or willful self-destruction; whatever violates the integrity of the human person, such as mutilation, torments inflicted on body or mind, attempts to coerce the will itself; and insults to human dignity, such as subhuman living conditions, arbitrary imprisonment, deportation, slavery, and prostitution. *255–256*

9. What is the basic purpose of human society and government according to the Catholic church?
Human society and government are to serve the individual person: safeguarding and promoting the human rights of each one and protecting against the threats to life itself. They also may assist in the realization of our final destiny. For example, we are required to support the common good in various ways (e.g., obeying traffic laws, paying taxes for services for all). At times citizens are called to serve in defense of justice or of the innocent—such as the harboring of Jewish people in World War II by Christians in Europe. A key example in our day involves recent efforts by Christians in the United States to overturn laws and court decisions that attack or threaten the sanctity of human life by allowing abortion and even euthanasia. *256*

10. Can Catholics isolate themselves from others in order to concentrate exclusively on their own personal salvation?
No. No one can ignore the needs of society or the church. Love of neighbor is just as essential to the Christian life as love of God (1 Jn 4:20, 21), and to love others we must first enter into social relationships with them. Christ desires that all people be saved (1 Tm 2:4), therefore we must also desire and work for the salvation of all. *257*

11. What is the primary role of the laity in the church?
Lay people are called to bring the Spirit of Christ into the daily affairs of human society through their own witness, their activities and abilities, so that the temporal order is transformed and renewed in Christ. This principle should underlie every Christian's attitude toward the world.

Some examples of the laity carrying out this task are: the businessman who conducts his dealings justly, the mother who cares for her children patiently, and the teenager who is responsible and prompt in carrying out his or her part-time job. *258, 269*

12. How are Christians to relate to the modern world?
They are not to submit themselves to the values or powers of the world that are opposed to God. Christians are to be involved in the world, but aware that this world is not their final end. Christians ought not be either "optimists" nor "pessimists" about the modern world. Instead, they should approach the world and human society with realism and Christian hope. For example, the poverty and famine in the world can seem overwhelming but each Christian can do much to alleviate misery through generosity in sharing money and possessions, and in living a modest lifestyle. *259*

13. How does Christian hope affect how we face situations in the world?
Christian hope affirms that all who consciously commit their lives to Jesus Christ and conform every area of their lives to his teaching will find peace and ultimate victory over all evil (Rom 8:22–25). *259*

14. How are Catholics challenged by the gospel and church teaching?
They are asked to sacrifice their lives (their time, energy, and money) so that the world and human society can be transformed according to God's will and plan. However, this can only occur if they first have been changed and transformed from within by the Holy Spirit. *259*

15. How can Catholics take active responsibility for the world?
There are different callings or vocations. Some are called to influence the world through a contemplative life of prayer and penance, like that in a religious order. Others are called to an active apostolate, like those called to be broadcasters or journalists who seek to introduce a Christian or moral perspective in their work. *259–260*

16. Is the contemplative vocation useless in today's world of action?
The contemplative life is not a passive approach or an escape from the world but a time-honored Catholic vocation based upon the realization that the course of human events is profoundly affected by prayer, as well as influenced by the prophetic lifestyle of the contemplative. The overemphasis on action common to Western society can flow from a lack of faith in the power of prayer. *260*

17. Do all Christians need to pray in order to work effectively?
Yes. Even those called by God to very active involvement in the world need to pray. We must know God's mind in order to act according to God's will, and we need his strength to sustain our efforts. Both of these come from personal and communal prayer. *260*

18. Is there any other reason why we should pray as well as work?
Yes. We also need to pray because there is spiritual opposition to the accomplishment of God's will in the world—opposition that can only be overcome by spiritual means and not by human effort alone (Mk 9:29; Eph 6:12, 18). *260–261*

19. How do Catholics bring Christ to the world?
There are two basic approaches: evangelization and seeking to transform the social order (including the political, economic, and cultural dimensions of human life). Both of these approaches are important for Catholics, but the first has priority. 262

20. Why should evangelization have priority over social action?
Society is made up of individual persons, and therefore will not reflect God's perfect will and Christian values fully unless the individuals who make up the society personally accept Christ as their Lord, and embrace the Christian way of life. 262

21. What is evangelization?
To evangelize means to bear witness to the reality of God's love shown in Jesus Christ and in the gift of eternal life that God offers to every person. 263–264

22. How does one witness?
To witness does not mean reciting doctrine or abstract truths. A witness has first-hand, personal knowledge of the reality to which he or she testifies. In order to evangelize, Catholics first must know the reality of God's love and of the power of the death and resurrection of Jesus Christ in their own lives. 264

23. Is the proclamation of the "good news" enough?
No. The Catholic church has always emphasized that the proclamation of God's word or the act of evangelization must be followed by an ever fuller instruction in the Christian life. Known as catechesis or *didache*, this involves teaching that contributes to the person's growth in holiness. 265

24. How does the church and its members seek to transform human society?

The history of the Catholic church abounds in examples of Catholics of every vocation starting works of mercy and other services as a response to the call of the gospel. Christ's ministry is carried on by his church through education, care of the sick, feeding the hungry, encouraging the lonely and discouraged, freeing the oppressed, and defending the rights of the poor, for example. 267

25. Can Catholics disagree about what are effective actions or responses?

Yes. There may be legitimate differences of opinion among Christians about specific actions to be taken or even disagreements in judging what is a truly Christian activity or response. Pope John Paul II and the Second Vatican Council have both taught that the gospel of Jesus Christ cannot be equated with any particular social, political, or economic system. 269

26. How do the pope and bishops assist the Catholic people to take action?

They give positive guidance and teaching from a Christian perspective to the members of the church about social issues and the concerns of the world. There have been numerous Catholic papal social teachings since Leo XIII's *Rerum Novarum* of 1893. And various individual bishops and national conferences of bishops have spoken out to give guidance to Catholics in particular areas.

The Catholic bishops have also set up and encouraged groups that work for justice and for the poor. They take up collections for the missions and urge lay people and religious to devote generously their lives and energies in various ways to the transformation of human society. 269

27. Has the church always held the same views and advocated the same responses?

Essential doctrines of the Catholic faith do not change, but the church's understanding of how it should relate to the world and apply its teaching to the life of human society does deepen and mature through the ongoing guidance of the Holy Spirit. *270*

28. What is an example of the growth or deepening of the church's social teaching?

In past centuries, the Catholic church advocated the establishment of the Catholic faith as the sole religion, where possible, with the enforcement of this by the state. The *Declaration on Religious Freedom* from the Second Vatican Council teaches that the best situation is one where individuals in a state have the freedom to choose and practice their religion freely (respecting the rights of all and the common good), with this freedom protected by the state.

29. Are there other areas in which the church teaching has not developed but has remained consistent over time?

Yes. For example, Catholic teaching regarding marriage and family life is one area in which church teaching has been strikingly consistent. This is an area of special concern for the church in the world today. *270*

30. Why is marriage and the family so important in the eyes of the church?

There are several reasons, but the most important is that marriage between man and woman is the sign or symbol of the bond of love between Christ and the church; it is the foundation of society and essential to the life of the church. The rising rate of divorce, the fragmentation of family life, abortion, artificial contraception, and other contemporary problems present serious challenges to Christian marriage and family life. All these reasons indicate that the church must take special care of this area in teaching and action. *271*

31. Why is the family the foundation of society?
Because it is the most basic social group. God wills for every person to enter the world and be prepared to participate in society through the family. *271*

32. Why is family life essential to the church?
It is from the family that new church members are presented for baptism, and within the family people are educated and trained in the knowledge and practice of their faith. Indeed, parents remain the primary teachers of faith and morality for their children. *272*

33. Why does the church teach that the marriage bond is sacred and indissoluble or permanent?
The marriage bond is a sign of Christ's love for the church which can never come to an end, because of its integral importance to a sound society, and because the family is "the domestic church" which reflects the unity of the entire church. *271–272*

34. Who established marriage?
God created the order and plan for married and family life as it is revealed through Scripture and in Catholic tradition. The basic order and plan for marriage is not subject to mankind's changes in culture or current philosophical thinking. *273*

35. How can Catholics grow in an understanding of God's order and plan for married life?
Catholics can and should study the Bible and Catholic tradition, particularly as summarized in the pertinent papal encyclicals of the last one hundred years. *273*

36. What other helps are available for Christian families to grow into all God desires for them?

Seeking out the support and encouragement from other Christian families with similar values can be a great help. Reading and studying sources based on authentic church teaching can help families practically apply the church's standards in their daily life. Involvement in sound movements aimed at renewal of family life within the church can achieve both of these objectives. 274

37. What is the mission of the Catholic family?

The Synod of Bishops in 1981 presented a four-fold mission of the Catholic family: 1) forming a community of persons; 2) serving life; 3) participating in the development of society; 4) sharing in the life and mission of the church. 275

NINE

Mary

1. Why do Catholics honor Mary at all?
Catholics honor Mary because God honored her by choosing her to be the mother of God incarnate, Jesus Christ (Lk 1:28). All Catholic doctrines concerning Mary are related to and emerge from our understanding of her Son, Jesus Christ. Mary has no significance for us apart from Christ. *278, 280*

2. Is there any mention of Mary's role in the Old Testament?
Mary's role in the coming of Christ was prefigured and foretold in the Old Testament. She is prophetically foreshadowed in the promise of victory given at the fall, where it is mentioned that the offspring of woman will crush the serpent's head (cf. Gn 3:15). Mary is, as well, the virgin who will conceive and bear a son, Emmanuel (cf. Is 7:14; Mi 5:2–3; Mt 1:22–23). She is among the poor and humble of spirit who await the coming of the Lord. She personifies the Daughter of Zion (Zep 3:14–15). *278*

3. What significance does Mary have in the New Testament apart from the birth of Christ?
Even though Mary is not spoken of at length or in great detail, she is mentioned at many of the crucial points of

the life of Christ and of his church, in addition to his birth. Her unqualified "yes" to the Lord at the annunciation (Lk 1:26–38) and her response of praise to God in the Magnificat (Lk 1:46–55) are models of discipleship for all believers. As the model disciple of the Lord, Mary reflects on God's saving action in her heart when she sees him work in her son's life in mysterious ways (Lk 2:51). The example of enduring hardships and sufferings (Mt 2:13–14; Lk 2:6–7; 2:35, 41–50) show that Mary was first and foremost a woman of faith in the midst of trials (Lk 2:19, 51). Mary appears as well at certain times during Jesus' public ministry (Jn 2:1–12; Mt 12:46–50; Mk 3:31–35; Lk 8:19–21). She was present at the foot of the cross and in the upper room at Pentecost (Jn 19:25–27; Acts 1:14; 2). *278–279*

4. Mary seems to have a much greater role in church tradition than she does in the Bible, why is this so?
Catholics believe that the Holy Spirit continues to unfold and deepen our understanding of the truths of faith found in the Bible. As a result of this process, the Catholic church has recognized and defined certain beliefs about Mary that are found implicitly in the Bible (not in their full form), doctrines which the universal church came to accept and believe with overwhelming consent through the guidance of the Holy Spirit. *280*

5. How can Mary be called the "Mother of God"?
The early church, led by the Holy Spirit, honored and addressed Mary as the Mother of God, *Theotokos* in Greek (literally God-bearer). They reasoned that if Jesus were truly God as well as man, and if Mary were truly his mother, it would be perfectly fitting to speak of Mary as the God-bearer, or Mother of God. His humanity came from the flesh of Mary while he always possessed his divine nature as the Son of God (Lk 1:35). Nonetheless, since

Mary gave birth to the *one person* of Jesus Christ, the Catholic church has held continually that Mary should be honored as the Mother of God. To claim otherwise would be to divide the person of Christ. *280–281*

6. Why do Catholics call Mary the "Virgin Mother"?

Since the fourth century and earlier, church leaders have taught that Mary remained a virgin throughout her life. Catholics believe that throughout her life, Mary abstained from sexual relations and bore no other children after the birth of Jesus. *281*

7. Doesn't it say in the Bible that Joseph knew her not until she had borne a son (Mt 1:25) and that Jesus had brothers?

The Greek word translated "before" or "until" does not imply that Mary had sexual relations with Joseph after the birth of Jesus. The use of the term "the brother" or "brothers" of Jesus is also ambiguous. The word could mean blood brothers, but it could also refer to other close relatives, such as cousins. Hence, the Bible neither clearly confirms nor denies that Mary remained a virgin. In such cases, Catholics have always sought to understand the Scripture according to what the Holy Spirit has led the church as a whole to believe. *281*

8. Why do Catholics refer to Mary as the mother of all Christians or the mother of the church?

Mary's perpetual virginity helps us to realize that through her call to be the mother of Jesus, Mary was also being called by God to be the mother of all Christians. On the cross, Jesus told John, "Behold your mother," as he had told Mary, "Woman, behold, your son" (Jn 19:26–27). The early Christians understood this event as a powerful symbol: Jesus gave Mary to be the mother of all his disciples, who are truly Jesus' "brothers and sisters." Mary, in this sense, is the mother of the church. *84, 282*

9. What is the immaculate conception?
This doctrine states that in view of Mary's role of bearing and raising the Son of God, God prepared her for this by freeing her from original sin from the moment of her conception in the womb of her mother Anne. God prepared Mary to be a vessel without a trace of sin, not because of her own virtue or merit but because of her unique role in the plan of salvation. She alone of all people who ever lived, had the privilege of bearing God himself, in his humanity, in her womb. *282*

10. If Mary was conceived without sin, did she really need a Savior?
The Catholic church teaches that Mary actually was the first to be saved by the grace of her Son Jesus. God first applied to Mary the grace that he knew and foresaw that Jesus would gain by his life and death on the cross. She was preserved from original sin by the grace of the Son of God, whom she would later bear in her womb. *282*

11. Does this doctrine state that Mary never sinned?
Mary was freed from original sin at the moment of her conception. Because she possessed free will and was tempted as we are, Mary had to choose to obey God and avoid sin as we do. Catholic tradition overwhelmingly affirms that Mary always responded to the grace of God to resist sin and thus remained without sin throughout her life. *283*

12. What about the apostle Paul's statement in Romans 3:23, "all have sinned and fallen short of the glory of God"? Doesn't this deny Mary's sinlessness?
First, it is clear that Paul is speaking about the norm, not

about exceptions, because certainly Jesus Christ himself was without sin. Second, the conclusion to this sentence in Romans (3:24) applies to Mary, who was preserved from sin by the merits of her Son, "they are justified by his grace as a gift, through the redemption that is in Christ Jesus. . . ."

13. What does the church mean when it says that Mary was "assumed" into heaven?

The doctrine of the assumption, formally defined in 1950, affirms that Mary experienced the resurrection of the body that is promised to all faithful followers of Jesus immediately at the end of her time on earth. Tradition does not authoritatively assert whether Mary died or was bodily assumed into heaven while still alive. In the Old Testament, we have accounts of both Enoch and Elijah being taken up into heaven by God while still alive (Gn 5:24 and 2 Kgs 2:11.) The assumption of Mary into heaven flows from and completes the concept of her immaculate conception. Since Mary was preserved from sin by a unique gift and grace of Christ, she was able to experience the immediate union of her whole being with God at the end of her earthly life. *284*

14. Does the assumption of Mary have any meaning for us personally?

It is a source of hope for us because it foreshadows what will one day happen to each faithful Christian. It anticipates what will happen at the final judgment to all who are to be saved: that we, too, will possess glorified bodies like Christ's and Mary's on the last day. *284*

15. Do we have to believe in these four doctrines?

Yes. Catholics are bound to believe these as articles of faith.

16. Is Mary a member, as well as the mother of the church?
Yes. Mary is not a goddess, but a fully human servant of God whom he has highly favored through his mercy and grace. She is a member, although unique and special, of the church. *285*

17. If she is a member of the church can we model ourselves after her?
Yes. Catholics honor Mary because she is the model disciple, the perfect, most faithful follower of her Son Jesus Christ. Thus, she is a model of true discipleship for each Christian. She is also a model for the church as a whole. *285–286*

18. Do Catholics worship Mary?
No, Catholics offer worship (*latria*) to God alone. Mary is given special veneration or honor (*hyperdulia*) because of her important role in God's plan of salvation.

19. Why do Catholics pray to Mary?
Catholics address Mary in prayer because we believe that God has given her to us as a mother who will always intercede for her children. We pray to Mary not to worship her, but to honor her for her fidelity to God and to ask for her intercession for our needs and that we might know and honor her Son Jesus more fully.

20. How can Catholics call Mary a "mediatrix" when Scripture says Jesus Christ is the one mediator between God and man (1 Tm 2:5)?
Jesus Christ is the one mediator between God and man, but Mary, as our mother, is committed to pray and intercede for each of her chidren and for the church as a whole. The Catholic church has long held that because of her sinlessness and close union with her Son, Mary has been

given a role of mediation or intercession before God above any other human being. In that role, Catholics speak of Mary as a mediatrix. *287*

21. Is there an example that will help explain how Mary can be a mediatrix?
Just as Jesus Christ is the one great high priest and we share in his royal priesthood, so too Jesus is the one mediator and we share in his mediation through our union with him. It is because Mary's union with Christ is so close that we use the term "mediatrix."

22. How is Mary a messenger of God?
At various times thoughout the church's history and notably more often in the past 150 years, appearances of Mary have been reported. In these apparitions, Mary usually presents a prophetic message. The message is often intended for the whole church or for a large segment of the church. This may indicate a time of urgency for Christians to repent and to respond to God's call. *287–288*

23. How does the Catholic church view these apparitions of Mary and their accompanying messages?
The church does not require its members to believe any Marian apparitions or particular messages are genuine since these are private revelation. These appearances must conform fully to the standard of public revelation if they are to be accepted and heeded. It is noteworthy that recent popes have visited and preached at some sites of Mary's reported appearances—such as Lourdes, France, and Fatima, Portugal—and that the messages of Mary presented at these and other sites have been judged by the Catholic church to be in full conformity with biblical teaching and authentic Catholic tradition. *288*

24. What does Mary say in these messages?

In the most widely accepted apparitions, Mary has consistently called Christians to prayer, repentance, and conversion to God. Sometimes she has warned of serious consequences for the world if this message remains unheeded. Mary always has presented herself in authentic apparitions as a messenger or servant of God. Although she has affirmed traditional Catholic titles for herself and encouraged the use of Marian prayers, such as the rosary, her focus is always unmistakably centered on her Son Jesus Christ. *290*

25. What kind of place should Mary have in the life of each Christian?

Mother Teresa of Calcutta has said that we should love Mary as Jesus loved her. The Catholic church recommends certain forms of honor and devotion, especially the rosary, prayed either individually or in families and groups; and the observance of the feasts of Mary, such as the Annunciation (March 25), the Assumption (August 15), the Immaculate Conception (December 8) and the Mother of God (January 1). Pope John Paul II has encouraged a special consecration of the world and individuals to Jesus through Mary. *290–291*

TEN

The Life of the Age to Come

1. Are we destined to live forever?
Yes. Our life here on earth is but a preparation for life after death. *293*

2. Does one earn, merit, or deserve eternal life with God?
No. Eternal life with God is an absolutely free gift.

3. What does mankind deserve apart from God's offer of grace?
Mankind deserves death because of original sin and our own actual sins flowing from this. The result of sin is death—eternal separation from God (Rom 6:23). *294*

4. How do we accept God's offer of grace which leads to salvation?
We accept salvation through our cooperation with God's grace and our freely given response to the work of the Holy Spirit in our lives. *294*

5. Does eternal life begin the moment we die?
Eternal life begins now in this life as we choose to respond to God and accept his gift of the Holy Spirit (Jn 17:3). *294*

6. How does this process begin in our lives?

The sacrament of baptism inaugurates this saving work in us (Col 1:13). We must believe in Jesus (Jn 3:16) and the Father (Jn 5:24), eat Jesus' flesh and blood in the Eucharist (Jn 6:54), and then follow Jesus, the Good Shepherd (Jn 10:27–28), throughout our lives. *294–295*

7. What should be the result of responding to God's call in this way?

A Christian should progressively become an entirely new creation (2 Cor 5:17) freed from the bondage of Satan and sin. This is what Catholics mean by "sanctification." *295*

8. What happens if we don't respond to God's offer of eternal life?

If we do not accept God's offer and continue to live in sin, then we experience even here on earth a foretaste of the pain of eternal separation from God. Sin, though it promises pleasure and fulfillment, never satisfies and actually leads to greater pain and misery. *295*

9. What should Christians fear?

The Bible consistently teaches that we should fear sin, not death (Mt 10:28). The result of sin is not merely physical death but the ultimate death of eternal separation from God and the pains of hell. *298–299*

10. How can we look forward confidently to receiving eternal life and happiness?

By the gift of hope. Hope is the fundamental virtue that enables Christians to look past the trials and struggles of this life and see all things with an eternal perspective (2 Cor 4:17; 5:1, 5; Jas 1:12). Sin no longer has power over those who know and follow Christ Jesus. He has conquered sin and along with it death (Rom 6:8–11; 8:1–2). *295–296, 299*

11. How should Christians view and approach death?
There is no need for fear for those who know the love of God (1 Jn 4:16–18). We should look at death with faith and hope (1 Thes 4:13, 14; Phil 1:23, 24; 2 Cor 5:6–9) since we believe in the resurrection of Jesus from the dead. *296–297*

12. Why does faith in the resurrection of Jesus provide Christians with such unshakable hope?
Christians believe that death is not a final end of life but a completion of the mission of life on earth. Resurrection from the dead is a reality that we will all experience. *298*

13. What is the goal of life?
It is primarily to come to know God through faith, hope, and love, so that the faithful may see him face-to-face after death (1 Cor 13:12, 13) and live joyfully in God's presence forever. As we begin to respond to God in this way, we enjoy his presence in this life too, although in a limited way. *298*

14. What is perfect and ultimate happiness?
The direct vision of God, traditionally called the "beatific vision," is the fulfillment of every human desire and longing. Until the second coming of Christ, this can only be fully attained by Christians by passing through death. While some saints have been shown heaven, their glimpse of it in this life has always been partial and limited. *298*

15. What happens at death?
The Catholic church teaches that at the moment of death, each person will come before the judgment seat of Christ to be judged on what they have done in their lives. This is known as the "particular judgment" in Catholic theology. *299–300*

16. Is this what is meant by the "last judgment"?

No. The last or general judgment happens at the close of human history when "Christ will come again in glory to judge the living and the dead" (Nicene Creed). *300*

17. What happens to those who have lived their lives fully in union with the Lord?

If they have repented of all sin and are unstained by sin's effects, then the moment of death will be a moment of glorious reunion with the Lord and the beginning of a life of unspeakable joy that will last forever. This state is called "heaven." *300*

18. What if someone dies in the grace of the Lord but with some remaining unrepented sin or the effects of sin still in their lives?

The Catholic church teaches that God, in his mercy, purifies the person of these sins so he or she can enter into the joy of heaven. This purification is known as "purgatory." *300, 306*

19. What happens to those who have rejected God when they die?

They receive the consequences of this choice beginning even at the moment of death: eternal separation from God which Jesus often called "hell" (Mk 9:47; Mt 18:7–9; Lk 16:19–31). *300*

20. What is hell?

Hell exists as an actual state or condition of being that lasts eternally (Mk 9:47–48; Mt 18:9). It may be a physical, material place since Christians believe in the resurrection of the body. The Catholic church has always been somewhat guarded in describing what hell is like, lest it succumb to exaggeration or inaccuracy. Both physical torment and interior mental suffering such as eternal despair, agonizing guilt, and full knowledge that the vision of God has been lost are referred to in Scripture (Mt 22:13; Lk 16:28; 3:17; 2 Thes 1:9; Rv 14:11–12). *304–305*

21. How can a good God create or permit a place like hell to exist?

Instead of asking why God could permit the existence of hell, we should rather ask why human beings could reject the all-good, all-loving God and his will. God has created us with free will. Hell and eternal damnation in hell are not God's ideas or will, but these sober realities are the consequences of free choices by his creatures, angels and humanity. *301–303*

22. Will many people end up in hell?

Jesus himself taught that the road to hell is broad and easy, and many will follow it (Mt 7:13–14). But the Catholic church does not officially teach that many or most people will end up in hell; that knowledge is reserved for God alone. *302*

23. How do we know if someone is in hell or in heaven?

The Catholic church teaches that we cannot judge or determine whether any particular person has been condemned to hell, even Hitler. The mercy of God is such that a person can repent even at the point of death and be saved, like the good thief crucified next to Jesus (Lk 23:39–43). *303*

24. What is "purgatory"?

Purgatory is God's way of completing the process of purification and healing from sin and its effects in this life—a process that begins here and now on earth. *307*

25. What is purgatory like?

The biblical images of purification from sin often speak of fire as the purifying agent. The Catholic tradition includes

the notion of purgation from sin by the fire of God's love
and holiness. Fire implies pain, and thus it should not
surprise us if purgatory is painful. Medical operations are
painful, but they effectively heal diseases. *307*

26. Why do Catholics believe in purgatory when it is not in the Bible?

Although the term is not found in the Bible, there are
some texts that refer to purgatory according to ancient
Christian tradition (2 Mc 12:46; 1 Cor 3:11–15). Catholics
believe that God's mercy is so great, his desire to save so
strong, and the infinite merit of Christ's death on the cross
for sinners is so powerful, that purgatory is God's saving
provision for those who die in the state of imperfect love.
306

27. How can this process of purification be aided for ourselves or others?

Through prayer and penance offered to God for the remis-
sion of sin, we can assist the purifying process for ourselves and others. This is the basis of the Catholic doctrine
of indulgences discussed earlier. *307*

28. Can we wait until purgatory to seek after holiness of life?

No. It would be wrong to presume that God will always
purify us after we die. Purgatory is not a "second chance"
to be saved for those who have rejected God's grace during their lives on earth. If we are not advancing in holiness
in this life, we are retreating from God. Purgatory is God's
provision for those who have sincerely sought to conform
themselves to his will yet die without full healing and
repentance from sin and its effects in their lives. *308*

29. What is heaven?

Heaven is sharing in divine life and joy to the extent that

we are drawn completely into the life of the Trinity (Jn 14:20). *310*

30. In heaven, do we lose our individual identities?
No. We find our true identity as we are immersed in God and his love. We are perfectly one with God and are perfectly ourselves as distinct individuals—just as the three persons of the Blessed Trinity are perfectly one and yet are three distinct persons.

31. Is heaven just a mental state of constant euphoria and contentment?
Catholics believe in the resurrection of the body, implying that heaven is a place and not just a vague state of existence. *310*

32. What is "limbo"?
Catholic theologians of the early church and the Middle Ages proposed the existence of a state of "natural blessedness" or happiness in which unbaptized infants would experience peace for eternity, but without the full joy of heaven. The Catholic church has never formally recognized nor denied the existence of limbo in its official teaching, though it does teach that baptism, in some form, is necessary for salvation. *310–311*

33. What period of history do we live in today?
We live between the first coming of Christ, when the kingdom of God has been inaugurated on earth, and his second coming in glory. *311–312*

34. What does this mean for the human race?
We are still free to ignore or to reject the kingship of Christ. Satan and his demons are permitted to attempt to draw people away from the reign of God and into their own dominion of darkness during this period of time. Con-

versely, this is a time in which Christians can respond to God's grace in order to advance God's kingdom on earth and to draw others into his kingdom through evangelization. 312

35. What will the second coming of Christ be like?
The second coming, or *parousia*, of Christ is described many times in the New Testament (Mt 7:15–23; 24:11–13; Mk 13:22; 2 Pt 2:1–3; 1 Jn 2:18, 22). The Bible indicates that a severe trial in the world, particularly for Christians, will immediately precede it. The Catholic church has never attempted to formally identify who the anti-Christ or anti-Christs will be, but they will cause many to fall away from true faith in Christ, and this activity will identify them. 312–313

36. Will the world situation be totally terrible and frightening before the Lord comes?
No. The Bible also speaks of a great age of evangelization throughout all the world immediately before the end (Mt 24:14). 313

37. How will we recognize when the Lord Jesus is returning?
Everyone will be be aware of Christ's return in glory; it will be an unmistakable event (Mk 13:26; Mt 24:30; Lk 21:27). He will come in great splendor and power, and his coming will fill the sky. 313

38. What will happen on earth when Jesus, the Son of man, comes?
It will be a time of judgment, when some will be gathered into God's kingdom, and others left behind (Mt 24:40–41). The Bible speaks of it as a time of great joy for faithful Christians, an exultant reunion (Lk 21:28; 1 Thes 4:16–18). 313

39. Do Catholics believe in the "rapture"?

Certain Protestant Christians refer to the lifting up of the elect in 1 Thessalonians 4:16–18 as the "rapture." The Catholic church does not define whether these images are to be taken literally or understood as poetic images or pointers to a reality beyond our imagination. *314*

40. When will the resurrection of the dead take place?

When Christ comes again, the dead will arise to receive their final reward or retribution. *314*

41. What happens after the second coming and final judgment?

These events mark the end of human history. Purgatory will also come to an end. The physical universe and earth will come to an end as we know it (Lk 21:33; 2 Pt 3:10–12; Rv 21:1). *314*

42. Will there be anything left except heaven and hell after that?

Yes. Scripture also contains the promise of a new heaven and a new earth (2 Pt 3:13; Rv 21:1), in which righteousness dwells and God will reign forever (Rv 21; 22). Our bodies will be raised and transformed as well as the physical universe (Rom 8:21). *314–315*

43. If everything is going to pass away what is the point of working to bring the world into conformity with the gospel?

Rather than negating our efforts, the promise of the transformation of all things enables and affirms our efforts. All good we do to promote the authentic values of human dignity, fellowship and friendship, freedom, and all the other good fruits of our labors will be found again without blemish—transformed—in the fullness of the kingdom of God. *315–316*

44. When will all these last things take place?

Both the New Testament and the Catholic church concur in one answer: we don't know. There are some signs that all should recognize, but the parables and direct statements regarding the exact time of Jesus' coming only indicate that his second coming will be sudden and unexpected (Mt 24:36, 43–44; Mk 13:32–33, 35–37; 1 Thes 5:2; 2 Pt 3:10). *316*

45. Are we living in the last days now and is the end of the world imminent?

Catholics believe that the final age of the world began (1 Cor 10:11) when Christ ascended into heaven. However, we do not state that the end of the world is imminent. The final coming of the Lord may or may not come during our lifetime, and none of us know the day nor the hour of our own death, our personal day of judgment. We must always be ready for the moment of our own death and for the end of the world. *316–317*

46. How should Catholics approach the last things?

Those who turn from their sins through ongoing repentance, who believe in Jesus Christ, and who obey his commandments through a life of daily discipleship, have nothing to fear on the day when Jesus Christ comes again to judge all. Christians who have faithfully followed Christ and have obeyed God's law do not need to face the end of the world or the final judgment with misgivings or fear but rather should look forward to it with expectation and hope (2 Pt 3:13; Rv 21; Lk 21:27–28). Maranatha! Come, Lord Jesus! *319–320*

Glossary of Terms Italicized in Text

Anamnesis: a remembrance or memorial that makes present a former reality, not just a mental recalling, or commemoration of a past event.

Annulment: an act by ecclesiastical authorities, usually a marriage tribunal, declaring that a marriage was never valid.

Apologetics: the branch of theology which explains doctrine and defends it against intellectual attacks.

Archbishop: a bishop of a large or important diocese or see. He has a special prominence because of the size or influence of his diocese, called an archdiocese.

Asperges: a ceremony during which the congregation and clergy are sprinkled with holy water in renewal of their baptismal vows.

Basilica: a title of honor, given by the pope, to certain churches noted for their antiquity or historical associations.

Benediction (of the Blessed Sacrament): a Roman Catholic church service during which the consecrated Host is placed in a monstrance on the altar. The purpose of this service is to adore Jesus Christ present in the Eucharist. The service concludes with a blessing (hence the name Benediction) of the people with the Host.

Blasphemy: insulting, mocking, false, or impious speech about God or other sacred matters. Blasphemy is a sin and, by its nature, a grave matter that must be confessed during the sacrament of reconciliation.

Canon: official list of recognized, authoritative writings, such as the books of the Bible, which are recognized by the church as inspired by God.

Cardinal: a bishop selected by the pope by virtue of outstanding holiness and service to God's people to help in the guidance and administration of the church. A cardinal is second in rank to the pope and belongs to the college of cardinals, which has a special advisory role to the pope. A special task of the cardinals is to elect a new pope.

Cathedral church: the church in which a bishop presides.

Celibacy: a vow not to marry and to renounce all sexual relationships in order to live a special life of service dedicated to Christ and his church.

Deuterocanonical: a second canon. The Catholic term for the writings of the Old Testament which are asserted as canonical by Catholics but considered apocryphal (not part of the Canon) by Protestants.

Evangelical Counsels: the vows of poverty, chastity (celibacy), and obedience. Those who have embraced the religious life usually take these vows and seek to live them out to the greatest degree possible.

Intercommunion: Christians of different denominations and traditions receiving Holy Communion together. This practice is forbidden among Catholics except in special cases with the express permission of the local bishop.

Magisterium: the teaching office or function of the pope and the bishops in union with him to pronounce, explain, and interpret matters of faith and morals. The Magisterium also has the duty to authoritatively interpret Scripture for the faithful when necessary.

Metropolitan: the title of a bishop exercising some authority over a province, not only a diocese. Many times a metropolitan is a cardinal or an archbishop, and dioceses within his care are called suffragans. The title is not commonly used in the Roman Catholic church.

Monsignor: a title bestowed upon a priest, usually by the pope, to honor him for distinguished service. This honorific title is not conferred often in English-speaking countries today.

Nature: the essence of something. Everything has essential components and properties that distinguish it from other things; those specifics form its nature.

Ordinary: the bishop who has primary responsibility for pastoring a diocese. This distinguishes him from retired bishops or from auxiliary bishops, who assist ordinaries.

Patriarch: a title usually used for the preeminent leader of an Eastern Catholic or Orthodox church. In the Roman Catholic church, the pope is the Patriarch of the West and certain metropolitans of venerable sees in the West do bear the title patriarch.

Person (in God): within the Trinity, "person" designates that which makes the Father, Son, and Holy Spirit different from each other, although they completely share the fullness of divine knowledge, freedom, and life (the divine "nature"). Specifically, this means that the Father is distinguished as a unique person by being the origin or source of all within the Trinity; the Son alone is a unique person as the perfect image or Word of the Father, who alone has become incarnate; and the Holy Spirit is the divine person who alone proceeds from the Father and the Son as the love uniting them, and as the divine gift poured out upon humanity by the Father and the Son.

Relations (in God): those things which distinguish the three divine persons of the Trinity and also those which unite them. The four divine relations are paternity (the relation of the Father to the Son), filiation (the relation of the Son to the Father), active spiration (the relation of the Father and the Son to the Holy Spirit), and passive spiration or procession (the relation of the Holy Spirit to the Father and the Son). These are all the relations of divine love by which the persons dwell within each other in perfect unity.

Substance: a being which possesses its own identity, "stands on its own." In theology, a substance need not be material, as when we speak of the Father, Son, and Holy Spirit, being "consubstantial," meaning "sharing the same (divine) substance," or that they are "one in being."

Triduum: a three-day prayer or celebration, public or private, especially in preparation for a feast. This is especially used in relation to Holy Thursday, Good Friday, and Holy Saturday.

Vestments: the garments worn by priests and bishops for the Liturgy of the Eucharist and other liturgical celebrations. Deacons wear vestments as well when assisting or presiding at liturgical celebrations.

Some Commonly Recited Catholic Prayers

APOSTLES' CREED

I believe in God, the Father almighty, creator of heaven and earth, and in Jesus Christ, his only Son, our Lord; who was conceived by the Holy Spirit, born of the Virgin Mary, suffered under Pontius Pilate, was crucified, died, and was buried. He descended into hell; the third day he rose again from the dead. He ascended into heaven, sits at the right hand of God the Father almighty; from thence he shall come to judge the living and the dead. I believe in the Holy Spirit, the holy Catholic Church, the communion of saints, the forgiveness of sins, the resurrection of the body, and life everlasting. Amen.

OUR FATHER

Our Father, who art in heaven, hallowed be thy name; thy kingdom come; thy will be done on earth as it is in heaven. Give us this day our daily bread; and forgive us our trespasses as we forgive those who trespass against us. And lead us not into temptation, but deliver us from evil. Amen.

GLORY BE

Glory be to the Father, and to the Son, and to the Holy Spirit. As it was in the beginning, is now, and ever shall be, world without end. Amen.

HAIL MARY

Hail, Mary, full of grace; the Lord is with you; blessed are you among women, and blessed is the fruit of your womb, Jesus. Holy Mary, Mother of God, pray for us sinners, now, and at the hour of our death. Amen.

THE FIFTEEN MYSTERIES OF THE ROSARY

(Each mystery is recited by praying one Our Father, ten Hail Marys, and one Glory Be, while prayerfully meditating on the meaning of the mystery.)

THE JOYFUL MYSTERIES

The Annunciation
The Visitation
The Nativity
The Presentation
The Finding of Jesus in the Temple

THE SORROWFUL MYSTERIES

The Agony in the Garden
The Scourging of Jesus
The Crowning with Thorns
The Carrying of the Cross
The Crucifixion

THE GLORIOUS MYSTERIES

The Resurrection
The Ascension
The Descent of the Holy Spirit
The Assumption
The Coronation of Our Lady

HAIL HOLY QUEEN

(The Hail Holy Queen is traditionally recited after praying the Rosary.)

Hail, holy Queen, Mother of Mercy. Hail, our life, our sweetness, and our hope. To you do we cry, poor banished children of Eve; to you do we send up our sighs, mourning and weeping, in this valley of tears. Turn then, most gracious advocate, your eyes of mercy towards us; and after this our exile, show unto us the blessed fruit of your womb, Jesus. O clement, O loving, O sweet Virgin Mary. Pray for us, O holy Mother of God. That we may be made worthy of the promises of Christ.

ANGELUS

(The Angelus is traditionally recited three times a day: early morning, midday, and evening.)

The angel of the Lord declared unto Mary: And she conceived of the Holy Spirit. Hail Mary . . . Behold the handmaid of the Lord: Be it done unto me according to your word. Hail Mary . . . And the Word was made flesh: And dwelt among us. Hail Mary . . . Pray for us, O holy Mother of God: That we may be made worthy of the promises of Christ.

FATIMA PRAYER

O my Jesus, forgive us our sins, save us from the fires of hell, lead all souls to heaven, especially those who are most in need of your mercy.

PRAYER TO ST. MICHAEL THE ARCHANGEL

(This prayer is particularly appropriate to recite when in need of spiritual protection.)

Holy Michael the Archangel, defend us in the day of battle; be our safeguard against the wickedness and snares of the devil. May God rebuke him we humbly pray; and may the prince of the heavenly host, by the power of God, thrust down to hell Satan and all wicked spirits, who wander through the world for the ruin of souls. Amen.

THE JESUS PRAYER

(The Jesus Prayer is helpful for meditative and repetitive prayer, especially in deepening our awareness of the presence and power of Jesus as the Savior.)

Lord Jesus Christ,
Son of the living God
Have mercy on me, a sinner.

GRACE BEFORE MEALS

Bless us, O Lord, and these your gifts which we are about to receive from your bounty, through Christ our Lord. Amen.

GRACE AFTER MEALS

We give you thanks for all your benefits (gifts), almighty God, who lives and reigns, for ever and ever. Amen.

THE MORNING OFFERING

O Jesus, through the Immaculate Heart of Mary, I offer you my prayers, works, joys, and sufferings of this day, for all the intentions of your Sacred Heart, in union with the Holy Sacrifice of the Mass throughout the world, in reparation for my sins, for the intentions of all our associates, for the reunion of Christendom, and in particular for . . . (mention your own intention).

THE EVENING OFFERING

O Lord our God, what sins I have this day committed in word, deed, or thought, forgive me, for you are gracious, and you love all men. Grant me peaceful and undisturbed sleep, send me your guardian angel to protect and guard me from every evil, for you are the guardian of our souls and bodies, and to you we ascribe glory, to the Father, and the Son, and the Holy Spirit, now and for ever and unto the ages of ages. Amen.

NIGHT PRAYER

Save us, O Lord, while waking, and guard us while sleeping, that when we wake, we may watch with Christ, and when we sleep, we may rest in peace. Amen.

STATIONS OF THE CROSS

(The Stations of the Cross, which recount the Lord's passion and death, are particularly appropriate to pray during the season of Lent.)

The first station: Jesus is condemned to death.

The second station: Jesus receives the cross.

The third station: Jesus falls for the first time.

The fourth station: Jesus is met by his blessed mother.

The fifth station: Simon of Cyrene helps Jesus to carry his cross.

The sixth station: Veronica wipes the face of Jesus.

The seventh station: Jesus falls the second time.

The eighth station: The women of Jerusalem mourn for our Lord.

The ninth station: Jesus falls for the third time.

The tenth station: Jesus is stripped of his garments.

The eleventh station: Jesus is nailed to the cross.

The twelfth station: Jesus dies on the cross.

The thirteenth station: Jesus is taken down from the cross.

The fourteenth station: Jesus is placed in the tomb.

COME HOLY SPIRIT

(This prayer is helpful to recite for personal spiritual renewal and for the renewal of the whole church.)

Come, Holy Spirit, fill the hearts of your faithful, and enkindle in them the fire of your love. Send forth your Spirit and they shall be created, and you shall renew the face of the earth. Let us pray. O God, who has taught the hearts of the faithful by the light of the Holy Spirit, grant that by the gift of the same Spirit we may be always truly wise and ever rejoice in his consolation. Amen.

INDEX

absolution, p. 81
angels, p. 15–16
ascension, the, p. 30, 37
astrology (the occult), p. 109
atonement,
   (*see* Jesus Christ, Death of)

bishop(s), p. 45–48, 61, 62–63,
   65–66, 72, 75, 81, 87, 115,
   116–117, 127

church, the,
   Catholic, p. 52–55, 123, 127
   definition of, p. 39, 43, 45–
     46, 52
   heirarchy of, p. 45–47
   nature of, p. 40–41, 70, 129
   salvation and, p. 52, 54
collegiality, p. 45
confession (or penance),
   (*see* sacraments, the: Reconcil-
     iation)
conscience, p. 83, 113–114, 116,
   117
conversion (repentance), p.
   106–107
covenant, p. 21–22, 26–27, 35,
   38, 79, 85
creation, p. 14–17, 28

deacon, p. 87–88
death, p. 19, 84, 139–142, 148
devil, the (Satan, Lucifer), p.
   15–16, 17, 19, 36, 107–109,
   145

devotions, p. 98–99
disciple, p. 31–33

ecumenical movement, p. 43–
   45
eternal life, p. 17, 27, 110, 139
evangelization, p. 126, 146
evil, p. 16, 18
evolution, church teaching on,
   p. 15, 17
Extreme Unction (or Last Rites),
   (*see* sacraments, the: Anoint-
     ing of the Sick)

fall, the, p. 17–19
final (last) judgment, p. 38
flesh, the, p. 19, 108
free will, p. 19, 21, 134, 143

goal of life, the, p. 105, 141
good news, the, p. 30, 58, 126
God, p. 17, 19–20, 67
   existence of, p. 11–12, 57
   Father, the, p. 28, 31, 69
   Holy Spirit, the, p. 37, 58, 80,
     124
   nature of, p. 12–14, 16
   Son, the, p. 27–29, 34
grace, p. 69–70, 71, 83, 86, 88,
   100, 111–113

heaven, p. 141, 142, 144–145,
   147
hell, p. 16, 19, 140, 142–143

Holy Spirit, the, p. 76, 101–103
  gifts of, p. 101–102
  fruits of, p. 101–102
  (*see also* God: the Holy Spirit)
humans, value of, p. 121–123

incarnation, the, p. 28–29
infallibility,
  bishops of, p. 47
  church, of the, p. 50
  pope, of the, p. 50
  Scripture of, p. 64–66
Israelites, the, p. 21–23, 24, 26

Jesus Christ,
  following, p. 32–33
  life, death, and resurrection
    of, p. 29, 34–37
  teaching of, p. 30–31, 52, 69,
    73, 77, 84, 85
  two natures of, p. 29
  virgin birth of, p. 28

laity, the (lay person), p. 51–52,
  123–124
law, p. 119
  divine, p. 117–118
  natural, p. 117–118
limbo, p. 145

Magisterium, the, p. 61, 66,
  116–117, 118, 119
marriage and the family, p. 119,
  128–130
  (*see also* sacraments, the: Mat-
    rimony)
Mary, p. 135
  apparitions of, p. 66, 137–138
  immaculate conception of, p.
    134–135
  mother (model) of the
    church, p. 42, 136
  other titles of, p. 132–133,
    136–137

perpetual virginity of, p. 133
  role (significance) of, p. 131–
    132, 138
Mass, the,
  (*see* sacraments: Eucharist,
    the)

Nicene Creed, p. 27–28, 43

pope, the, p. 48–50
prayer, p. 91–92
  liturgical (communal), p. 92–
    97
  personal, p. 92, 98–99
priests, p. 47, 51, 72, 81
  (*see also* sacraments, the: Holy
    Orders)
prophets and prophecies, p.
  24–27
purgatory, p. 100–101, 142,
  143–144

real presence, the, p. 77, 78
religious life, p. 51, 52
resurrection, the, p. 36–37, 80
revelation,
  divine (supernatural), p. 11,
    13, 14, 22, 57–59, 68, 118
  natural, p. 11, 57
  private, p. 66–67
  public, p. 58–59
rosary, the, p. 99

sacramentals, p. 99
sacraments, the, p. 69–72
  Anointing of the Sick, p. 84–
    85
  Baptism, p. 72–75
  Confirmation, p. 75–77
  Eucharist, the, p. 77–80, 93,
    95–96
  Holy Orders, p. 86–89
  Matrimony, p. 85–86
  Reconciliation, p. 80–84

saint(s), p. 41–42, 97–98
salvation, p. 21–22, 25, 27, 32–
    33, 52–54, 65, 112, 123, 139
Scripture, p. 25–26, 58–59, 61–
    66, 67–68, 92, 95–96, 118–
    119, 132
second coming, the (of Christ),
    p. 38, 145–148
sin, p. 17, 34–36, 81–83, 139–
    140
   mortal, p. 82–83
   original, p. 18–19
   venial, p. 83
situation ethics, p. 115

Ten Commandments, the, p.
    23–24
tradition, sacred, p. 59–61
Trinity, Blessed, p. 13–14

virgin birth, the,
   (*see* Jesus Christ: virgin birth
   of),
virtues, p. 12, 109–111
vocation(s), p. 85, 125

works of mercy, p. 111, 127
world, the, p. 107–108, 121–
    122, 124–128, 146